Interpreting Disability

Interpreting Disability
A Church of All and for All

Arne Fritzson and Samuel Kabue

WCC Publications, Geneva

Cover design: Marie Arnaud Snakkers
Cover photo: WCC/Peter Williams

ISBN 2-8254-1393-3

© 2004 WCC Publications
World Council of Churches
150 route de Ferney, P.O. Box 2100
1211 Geneva 2, Switzerland
Web site: http://www.wcc-coe.org

No. 105 in the Risk Book Series

Printed in Switzerland

Table of Contents

Preface

This book is written against the backdrop of the revitalization of disability work within the World Council of Churches, with emphasis on inclusion, full participation and active involvement in the spiritual, social and developmental life of the church. It comes just after the 2003 release of the WCC's second theological statement on disability which has highlighted key themes of commonalities and differences, the hermeneutical issue, *imago Dei*, healing and forgiveness, giftedness and "a church for all". These themes raise fundamental theological principles, a few of which are explored in this book from an experiential point of view by the authors.

The first part of the book, by Arne Fritzson, is written from the perspective of an ordained male person from the North who lives with a disability. He explains his experience as a minister of the church, a theologian and a scholar, and tries to show how disability has impacted his experiences. He takes the reader through his analysis of some of the theological themes mentioned above and their interpretation in the real lives of persons with disabilities.

The second and third parts of the book are written by Samuel Kabue, an African lay person with a disability and a strong leaning to church advocacy work. The second part in particular communicates a very personal dimension of disability experience within the context of the society in general and the Christian faith in particular. This section explores the question of attitude and prejudicial treatment of people based purely on perceptions of their place in society. Exploiting some of the themes dealt with in part one, the section makes an analysis of misconceived ideas of whether one is or is not capable as a result of his or her impairment. The section attempts to explain the changes necessary in society and the church to bring about full participation and active involvement and the contribution of gifts that those considered weak can make. It also demonstrates how persons with disabilities are relegated to roles of unfortunate beings at the receiving end of charitable impulses.

The third section of the book explores the growth and development of global disability work. It conducts the reader through the historical development of the provision and passive reception of services, to a renaissance marked by the growth and development of a vibrant disability movement. It also explores the United Nations' role in disability rights debates and interventions. Lastly, it traces the ecumenical response to disability over the decades up to the WCC's current work under the Ecumenical Disability Advocates Network, a means of addressing disability within the Justice, Peace and Creation programme. In the process, this third section of *Interpreting Disability* introduces the World Council of Churches' interim theological statement, "A Church of All and for All".

Definitions

The term "disability" is a creation of modern society in its attempt to group people with different characteristics perceived to have related or similar effects on human life. It is not a term that existed either in the Western or the African traditions. The Judaeo-Christian tradition did not have this type of classification as it described individuals as suffering from specific infirmities. This explains why the term is not to be found in the Bible. It emerged in the context of an attempt to have organized care for people who in the eyes of the society were seen to require looking after. The earliest definitions of the term were therefore offered by care-givers. Arguments over definitions have intensified with the emergence of new players in the field. Thus, "disability" has been defined in different ways at different times and by different categories of people. These definitions have reflected different interests and understandings depending on who may have been defining it. The definitions fall into two main classifications, namely, the medical model and the social model. Care-givers, health workers and academics have largely embraced the medical model while persons with disabilities through their movements largely are proponents of the social model.

Persons with disabilities argue that there is a hidden political purpose behind the definition of care-givers –

which is to justify their own roles. Their definitions are backed up by political and academic supporters who rely on them for advice. On the other hand, there is also an important political task embraced by the people-with-disabilities movement as a social group. This is to gain control over the way their situation is described and defined. A commonly prevailing view among persons with disabilities, especially in Britain and Western Europe, is that "medical" definitions locate the cause of the problems faced by persons with disabilities in their individual impairments. It is argued that as long as care-givers maintain the idea that it is the bodies of those with disabilities that are at fault, traditional social structures created by generations of care-givers can be protected. By the simple device of focusing on the "patients'" bodies, these definitions draw attention away from a discriminatory society. Such definitions underpin the dominant hegemony of ideas constructed to justify the care-giver's position.

Typical of definitions devised according to the medical model are those that were once put forward by the World Health Organization (WHO):

Impairment: Any loss or abnormality of psychological, physiological or anatomical structure or function.

Disability: Any restriction or lack, resulting from an impairment, of ability to perform any activity in the manner or within the range considered normal for a human being.

Handicap: A disadvantage for a given individual, resulting from an impairment or disability, that prevents the fulfilment of a role that is normal depending on age, sex, social and cultural factors for that individual.

The emergence of fresh thinking and new organizations controlled by people with disabilities themselves, and their struggle against segregation, has resulted in a careful reworking of this set of definitions. The resulting definitions are similar to those of the WHO, but are seen as a direct challenge by people with disabilities:

Impairment: Lacking all or part of a limb, or having a defective limb, organ or mechanism of the body.

Disability: The disadvantage or restriction of activity caused by contemporary social organization which takes no or little account of people who have physical impairments and thus excludes them from participation in the mainstream of social activities.

The political significance of these definitions lies in the fact that they are statements coming out of the direct experience of disability; that they place the cause of disability fairly and squarely with society; that they separate and sharpen the distinction between the individual and the environment within which he or she interacts; that they are a tool for measuring the role and relevance of existing service systems; that they pose disability positively as a phenomenon which can be overcome; and that they lift the veil which obscures the ugly face of discrimination in contemporary society against people with disabilities.

In ecumenical circles, descriptions of disability have moved from the realm of theological reflection to practical questions of inclusiveness within churches and church communities. Terms such as "persons with handicaps" and "the differently abled" and "persons with a disability" have been used at different times and usually have been designed to reflect inclusiveness as each replaced the other. The term "the differently abled" was used over a long time during the World Council of Churches' most active period of disability work. It had to be discarded because it was understood only within the ecumenical family and especially in churches and organizations closely related to WCC. There is still some remnant of it among certain groups within the ecumenical family. However, the terms in use at the WCC since 1997 have been "persons with disabilities" or "people with disabilities". With the unfolding interpretation and understanding of disability by different sets of players, these terms are already considered inappropriate if not controversial in some circles. Perhaps this is as it should be in order to encourage ongoing discourse which may lead to deeper understanding of the reality behind different descriptive phrases.

Disability and Meaning

Arne Fritzson

To write a book is a pretentious thing. It is to make a claim to have a story to tell. This book is about the concerns of people with disabilities, and it is about the Christian faith. Why should I, of all persons, tell you something about these things?

I am a person with a disability, cerebral palsy, and I am a Christian, an ordained pastor in a small, reformed Swedish free church – the Mission Covenant Church of Sweden. I am also a male, married, Western, academically trained, white person with a middle-class background. I belong to that tradition that for too long a time has claimed to do basic *theology* while others are doing special forms of "theologies". And there are a lot of Christians who live with different forms of disabilities. So why should I, of all people, write about disability and Christian faith? Now, when the World Council of Churches (WCC) provides a space for this important conversation, why should I occupy that space? I, who belong to a culture of colonizers, even though my country had a very small part in the history of European colonization? Am I too a colonizer when I claim this arena to put forward my thoughts on this important subject? Are there not more important voices to be heard? Voices that for too long were silenced, people whose stories need to be told and heard?

This could be interpreted as an overly defensive, self-justifying, way to start a book. But that is not the intention. I do believe that there are complications impeding my project of writing this book. Nonetheless, I am writing. After all, whoever might have written this book could be accused of colonizing this space; so why not me, in spite of my background? I never chose to belong to a category that has been privileged at others' expense, even though history may have had it that way. So why not take this opportunity to express my views and do it with vigour and pride, and pretend that all the problems I have mentioned do not exist, even though I know that they are real and pressing? A lot of people choose to handle these problems of interpretation by ignoring them, seemingly as a way of giving up the possibility of handling them in other and more cautious ways. Sometimes writers use expressions such as "doubtless" or "certainly" to enforce what they are saying, as though such devices will prevent criticism.

I do not believe there is a way to transcend the particularity of an author's experience. But I do believe that there is a more fruitful way to handle it than just to ignore it. In fact, this is what the current text is all about. It is written out of the conviction that the fact that we all come out of different contexts and have different stories creates a gap between us that we never fully bridge. Our bodily constitutions make it impossible for us fully to understand life from another human being's perspective. We literally cannot walk in others' shoes; even so, it is possible for us to share fragments of understanding and at least partially to grasp others' experiences of what it is to live as a human being in God's world.

We can share fragments, nothing more, nothing less. This means that an expression will have a different meaning for you than it has for me. We cannot fully understand each other, at least if we try to discuss existential questions. Consequently, we should have an attitude that is both critical and generous, both humble and proud, both in writing and reading. It must be generous and humble so we respect the one with whom we are communicating, and critical and proud so we dare to communicate what is important for us and critically discern what we receive, not accepting everything we are told.

I am raising a hermeneutical question, a question about interpretation, and this is natural for someone like me who has a special interest in hermeneutics. Academic discourse has rightfully been criticized for often being too insensitive to different contexts and claiming to speak about one universal human experience. While I will try to do what I can to avoid that mistake here, this academic discourse is part of my context and as such I will use it as a resource for my thinking.

However, there is yet another and perhaps more important reason for me to turn to hermeneutics when working with this issue, namely, that the question of disability has a crucial and quite complicated hermeneutical dimension. In many conversations I have had, I have noticed that talk of disability often leads to misunderstandings. I have come to believe that these misunderstandings usually arise from different interpretations of disability. That is why I believe that we need a hermeneutical framework for the issue of disability, and in this section of this book I will humbly suggest how such a framework may be developed.

My hermeneutic model is a fairly simple one. It draws from the thinking of Hans-Georg Gadamer and Paul Ricoeur. The model builds on the observation that when we as human beings try to understand each other, we can do it out of at least two different perspectives. On the one hand, we can start from the perspective of likeness, that we as human beings are fairly similar to one another and that we can recognize ourselves in our fellow human beings. So we can see our own needs and vulnerability in the person we meet. This is consistent with the golden rule that Jesus taught us: whatever you want others to do to you, you too shall do to them (Matt. 7:12). This teaching is based on the assumption of likeness. It assumes that you can understand others' human needs by asking how you would like to be treated if you were in a similar situation. Classical statements on the right of human beings such as the French revolutionary "Rights of Man" or the UN's universal declaration on human rights are also based on the assumption that we are alike and have similar needs that need to have similar protections.

But the other possibility for understanding one another starts with the opposite assumption: that we as human beings are different from each another. We have different backgrounds, different experiences, we live under different circumstances. From that perspective it is more complicated to believe that we can understand each other on the basis that one recognizes oneself in one's neighbour. Because the neighbour might have other needs, and, by treating her or him as one would like to be treated, one may be pushing the neighbour into a position that he or she does not want to be in. The rise of different forms of contextual theology in the latter part of the 20th century was based on this approach to understanding the other. It was partly a reaction against a Western white male theology that started in a presumed common human experience defined from a position of privilege. My conviction is that theological reflection must begin with the particularities of every human being.

Both these approaches have been challenged from different perspectives. I have already mentioned the critique of contextual theologies concerning much Western theology. This is one part of a larger movement that is criticizing the whole idea that we can talk about human commonalities. The idea of universal human rights came out of a French bourgeois revolution that drew only from the experiences of a small segment of that society. Can we really base our understanding on a presumed likeness among human beings?

One school of theory that clearly does not asssume this is Marxism. According to that ideology different people have different relations to the means of production, and from that follow different interests and different understandings. According to Marxist theories, our differences cannot be bridged. That is why such theorists tend to see a violent conflict between different interests as unavoidable. One need not be a Marxist to be challenged by this epistemological assumption. Is it possible to presume that we as human beings have so much in common that we can expect people to understand each other? On the other hand, is it possible to live without assuming any kind of common ground between us humans? What would happen to ethics, politics and our way of communicating if we did not assume common ground? Would the notion of empathy be totally empty?

My conviction is that both assumptions, that is, the one for likeness and the one for differences, lead to absurd consequences if they are driven to their extremes, if we presume that either one of them is totally right and the other is totally wrong. We need to find a compromise between the two if we are to construct a way to approach each other that is both intellectually viable and ethically responsible. The problem is, what should such a compromise look like?

The problem that this book attempts to address is how to understand disability in view of the foregoing hermeneutical questions. I believe that the solution to that problem is far from obvious, and how we handle it has a major influence on how we interpret life with a disability. I believe that a major reason for misunderstandings when people discuss questions relating to disability is that their reflections start from different assumptions about what it is to be a human being in God's world: some start from the assumption of likeness, others from the assumption of differences. This initial discrepancy is crucial when we talk about our understanding of disability in relation to Christian faith. Clarity in this matter is urgently needed. My hope is that this text can contribute to achieving such clarity.

Can the Bible settle this for us?

Is the whole question of likeness and difference between human beings really a problem for Christian theology? Can the Bible settle it for us? Has scripture no clear guidance to offer us? My answer is: None at all. We find the same ambiguity that I have already described in the scripture. The very first verses in Genesis that mention human beings (1:26-28) include both unity and diversity. Humanity is created in God's image. Every human being has that in common. But in that very unity lies diversity, reflected in the fact that we are created different as men and women. Genesis goes on to tell about Adam, and the fact that "Adam" is not a proper name but the Hebrew word for "mankind" shows us that this narrative tells us something about every human being. But the story also introduces differentiation between sexes as a part of God's intention for humanity.

The first eleven chapters in the Bible tell of the hostility that differentiation among human beings creates; for example, in the story about Cain and Abel or about Noah and the flood. The story of the tower of Babel shows how God creates a differentiation among human beings in order to save them from themselves. In the twelfth chapter of Genesis, God makes a differentiation between Abram and his children, on the one hand, and all the rest of humankind on the other. Yet even that differentiation, we are told, has implications for the whole of mankind. What happens to the people of Abram has consequences for every people on earth.

In the New Testament there is the same complexity. We have many passages that speak of unity. One example is John 17 and another is Ephesians 4. We also have passages that speak of lack of unity as a sin; for instance, the party spirit St Paul mentioned in 1 Corinthians 1-3. But this New Testament unity is a unity in diversity. In 1 Corinthians 12, St Paul explores the metaphor of the Christian community as a body with many limbs and organs. Paul invites his readers in the disharmonious Corinthian church to imagine parts of one body attempting to live as though they do not need each other. Or again, could they imagine if the whole body were made up of eyes only? That is quite an absurd image. But just as absurd as a body that is made up only of eyes is the image of a Christian congregation without any differences. Not even the biblical predictions of the *eschaton*, or end-time, answer whether scripture's ultimate vision for mankind is of unity or differentiation. Some passages talk about unity; for instance, 1 Corinthians 15:22. But many others talk about a differentiation. One example is Revelation 7:9. So we cannot turn to the scripture for a simple answer as to which is the correct basic assumption, likeness or difference.

But what about disability?

What is the relationship between the question of likeness or difference and the issue of disability? At first, this may seem a fairly simple question. After all, we use the word "disabled" to name a special group of persons as opposed to others who are not disabled, those who are able-bodied, temporarily able-bodied or what we shall call "the other group".

The concept of disability implies differentiation. But the question is much more complicated than that.

We can choose to interpret disability from a perspective that is common to human experience. Disability adds something to a person's life. From that understanding, a possible strategy to tackle concerns of persons with disabilities could be labelled normalization. Another possible way to interpret disability is to see it as one among many ways to live. In this understanding, there is no normal way for humans to live. The notion of normalization will in this understanding be, at best, pointless, but it could even be viewed as oppressive. In this understanding, persons with disabilities may be understood as one minority group among many minority groups. Of course, that does not mean that persons with disabilities do not have anything in common with other human beings. But these factors are regarded as secondary when trying to understand what living with disability means.

Likeness

Let us explore in more detail what these two ways of understanding disability mean, and what effects each has in our practical everyday lives with disabilities. I will start by exploring the model of interpretation that proceeds from the assumption of a basic likeness between human beings with or without disabilities. That is not an innocent choice. Whichever understanding I choose will dictate a pattern of priority, ranking one set of concerns over the other. I start with likeness because I believe that this is the traditional way of understanding disability, at least in Western societies, and historically that understanding has shaped much of our thinking around disability.

Traditionally, disability has been interpreted as a loss, as something that has demonstrated the inherent tragedy of human life. In some cultures we find other ways of interpreting disabilities, where, for example, persons with disabilities are seen as carriers of special gifts, but that has not been the case in most of Western culture. Disabilities have been interpreted as a divine punishment for sins committed by earlier generations. They also have sometimes been understood as the consequence of demonic activity. A northern European superstition held that human infants might be stolen from their cribs by evil spirits, and replaced with "changelings". Some parents concluded that children with disabilities must have been the result of such a substitution. Tragically, many babies froze to death when their parents left them in the forest, hoping that supernatural beings might return a "real", able-bodied son or daughter. In Western societies persons with disabilities were seen as "rightly poor", which meant that they themselves were not responsible for their poverty, as opposed to the wrongly poor. This view was based on an understanding that disability is something that falls short of fully human life. Even though that did not have to mean that persons with disabilities were not fully human, it did mean that their conditions of life were interpreted as tragic and less fulfilling than others'.

Towards the end of the 19th century a new approach to disability grew strong in Western societies. It was an optimistic understanding based on the assumption that if persons with disabilities were exposed to the right forms of pedagogical treatment they would function as able-bodied. This was the beginning of the large institutions. It was an interpretation built on the assumption of likeness. With hard training, persons with disabilities could become "normal". The pride taken by society in these institutions was manifested through the architecture in which they were built: many of them were conceived in a monumental style.

The optimism of the period of institutionalization over time was followed by a much more pessimistic and oppressive period. In the 1930s persons with disabilities were understood as chronically ill and dangerous to society. According to this understanding, they were a threat to healthy people. Thus, the rationale for institutions, from one of changing conditions for the better, became one of protecting the rest of society from dangerous individuals. In my own country, Sweden, a large number of persons with disabilities, mostly women, were sterilized during this period. Those sterilizations were often labelled as voluntary but were in practice a precondition for being permitted to live outside the institutions. This tragic period in our history meant that society had developed an understanding that had a great emphasis on the difference between persons with disabilities and the rest of the population. That difference was understood as static – persons with disabilities could not change, and they posed a threat that society needed to protect itself from by any appropriate means. That is why I categorize this understanding of disability under the headline "likeness", even though it stresses differences. Differences were regarded as dangerous to society, so the aim was to achieve social likeness even at the cost of using violence.

This sad period eventually was followed by a new one notable for the introduction of a new terminology. The word "handicap", a term from the world of sports, now came to be used in relation to disability. Over time, we in Sweden have combined this word with other terms. We talk about handicap policy, handicap organizations, handicap sport, handicap research, etc. Even now, when we have stopped using the word "handicapped" as a label for persons with disabilities, we still live with all those combinations. For instance, in Sweden we talk about a handicap movement and not a disability movement. Maybe this is due to the fact that the former word is much easier to say in Swedish. The future will reveal whether the word will disappear from our language. There are signs that this might be the case.

At about this time, new political goals were set for the society's approach to people with disabilities. "Normalization" and "integration" became the political goals of the "handicap policies". We have to remember that this was the time of the large institutions and "normalization" represented a significant change in the lives of the residents in those settings; for example, the right to have a normal week and a normal year. Every day was no longer the same, 365 days per year, but weekdays came to differ from weekends and summer meant a vacation from everyday routines. Many areas of life, such as education, work and family life were affected by this normalization policy.

This policy put a strong emphasis on likeness. Persons with disabilities were to become like the rest of the population, those who were regarded as "normal", and integrated among them. The factors that stopped persons with disabilities from becoming normal should be removed. Persons with disabilities should become a part of everyday life in society. During this period, churches' involvement in the lives of persons with disabilities also began to change. There was talk about integration in the churches in Sweden. Earlier the churches had met persons with disabilities at institutions when church people came and had a special worship for them. Suddenly, persons with disabilities could be a part of the ordinary congregation gathering for Sunday worship, or of the church-sponsored scout or youth groups. This became a challenge to the design of the churches' physical facilities. The need for accessibility for wheelchair users slowly started to be felt in some churches. Even if accessibility in the pews is nowadays good in most Swedish churches, there often are a few steps in the front of the churches that prevent the full participation in the churches' spiritual lives for many persons with disabilities.

A new theological understanding

This new understanding meant that the traditional theological interpretation of disability was challenged. Earlier people with disabilities were seen as a weak group that needed to be taken care of. They were the ones that received what other people gave. In a way, it is possible to say that people with disabilities, as such, had a function in the churches. As Christians, the people of the churches felt the need to do good things, to demonstrate their own goodness. And so, people with disabilities became objects of the churches' need to do good deeds.

With the new understanding of disability, manifested in the fact that the term "handicap" came in to use, new questions were put concerning the churches' approach to people with disabilities. Should people with disabilities always be the ones who receive what the people around them choose to give? Could they adopt another role in the lives of the churches? Discussion was generated in regard to the special gifts given to people with disabilities, and it was conceded that they as a group had a mission within the churches. The language of the ecumenical movement was applied in these discussions. Is the one body of Christ whole without people with disabilities? If we have one Lord, one faith, one baptism, one God and Father of all (Eph. 4:5-6), what does that say about the churches' approach to people with disabilities?

With the new understanding of disability the New Testament language of weakness, especially articulated in the two epistles to the Corinthians, came into focus. What does it mean that God chose what is weak in the world to shame the strong (1 Cor. 1:27)? What of the words that "the parts of the body which seem to be weaker are indispensable" (1 Cor. 12:22)? Notice that St Paul here writes "seem to be" and not "are". Consider the strange words that the Lord gave St Paul in 2 Corinthians 12:9, "My grace is sufficient for you, for my power is made perfect in weakness." Do they have any import when the churches reflect on their response to people living with disabilities? Can a church that is not open to the gifts from the parts of the body that seem weaker learn where the power of the Lord is made perfect?

When our theological understanding of the issues of disability is related to the language of weakness in the epistles to the Corinthians, then it connects with the very centre of Christian faith, Easter and the resurrection. Easter is the context in which St Paul elaborates the theme of weakness, as made clear from the words in 2 Corinthians 13:4: "For he was crucified in weakness, but lives by the power of God. For we are weak in him, but in dealing with you we shall live with him by the power of God." When we are trying to interpret the passages on weakness in the two epistles to the Corinthians, it is important to know about social tensions within the congregation. There, people from different social layers meet who hardly ever interact with each other in the society outside, at least not on the basis of equality. One problem is that members of the church have dramatically different financial resources, a circumstance reflected in the passage on the Lord's supper in 1 Corinthians 11:20-30. These passages represent a dialectic between strength and weakness. As the words "seem to be weaker" in 1 Corinthians 12:22 indicate, it is not obvious what is strength and what is weakness. What St Paul tells us is that we cannot discover our strength without acknowledging our weaknesses.

For many persons within churches around the world, this theme of weakness has been an inspiration for involvement in the disability issue. It has changed the question from what the churches can give people with disabilities to what people with disabilities can give the church. With this shift, a kind of equality has entered the discussion around the churches' way of meeting people with disabilities. New questions arose concerning people with disabilities and their involvement in the lives of the churches. For instance, can persons with a disability become spiritual leaders in a church? Can they enter the ordained ministry? For many churches, these were found to be hard questions and the answer was not always obvious. A lot of persons with disabilities felt hurt by the way churches handled such issues.

With a new understanding, interpretation of disabilities starting from an assumption of likeness comes to a new, and perhaps final, phase. Although the focus shifts to the term "weakness", this new understanding still makes the assumption that there is a norm for what human beings are and that persons with disabilities differ from this norm. With this criticism, new questions arose in the theological discourse on people with disabilities: Do we have to take a much more radical step in order to find a theological understanding of disability that is not oppressive towards people with disabilities? Do we have to abandon the assumption that there is something basic that we have in common as human beings?

Must our understanding begin with the fact that we as human beings are different from one another?

Differences

Is the assumption of likeness realistic? The movement of contextual theologies during the latter part of the 20th century helped us to see how deeply problematic that assumption is. To presume to know something because all humans are similar is to claim a lot. What is a human being? Someone with two arms and two legs? No! Someone with certain cognitive skills, such as the capacity to think in a reflective manner? No! Both of those definitions exclude a lot of human beings and are therefore oppressive. And in such a way, many descriptions of what human beings have in common may be over-ruled.

Part of the problem is due to the nature of human language. The intellectual progression of 20th century philosophy has made us aware of the fact that language is, in itself, problematic. In language we do not mirror reality but interpret it. Human language is not transparent. As human beings, we interpret the same things differently. A linguistic expression has the potential to mean different things to different persons. We say that it has a surplus of meaning. What does this imply for issues of people with disabilities in general, and for our theological understanding of those issues in particular. For instance, how can we now relate to the notion of weakness? Who determines who is weak and who is strong? If we label a certain group weak, do we then impose our understanding of weakness on another person? Is this an expression of intellectual imperialism?

These questions have formed the background to developments through which we have seen theologians develop a new theological understanding of disability that questions the language of weakness. That language locks people with disabilities into the position of weakness. But they should be strong and define the conditions for their own lives. As people with disabilities they should decide for themselves how their lives should be interpreted. The traditional interpretation of disability as something tragic needs to be challenged. The language of loss needs to be replaced by a more constructive, liberating language. God has made human beings different, with different sexes, colours, backgrounds. Is disability a part of natural differentiation? Can people with disabilities be proud of their lives, conditions and the contributions they can bring to humanity?

With the search for a new, liberating approach to disability it was important to address the question of which terminology to use. Distinctions were made between the terms "impairment", "disability" and "handicap". "Impairment" refers to a different functioning for an individual or group of individuals than what is considered "normal". "Disability" describes the consequences of the impairment; that is, inability to perform some tasks that are considered necessary. "Handicap" denotes a social disadvantage that the disability causes.

For some of those working in this direction, the distinction between congenital and acquired disability has been important. Of course, a disability has a different impact in your life depending on when you acquired it. If the disability is congenital, you have always lived with it and it has formed your identity. In a Swedish film, a man with cerebral palsy was asked if he would want to have his impairment if he was given the chance to live his life a second time. "Without it I would not be me," was his reply. But if you have built up an identity without a disability and acquire one later in life, you need to go through a process of adjustment both emotionally and in the way you organize your life. You have to come to terms with the fact that you lost a function you used to have. How much this distinction should influence our basic understanding of disability is debatable.

An important tool for this way of interpreting disability was the minority group model that holds that a minority group is a group of people who, because of their physical or cultural characteristics, are singled out from others in society for different and unequal treatment, and who therefore regard themselves as objects of collective discrimination. The minority group understanding of people with disabilities has proved to be an important concept for seeing the need for political changes to improve conditions of living for people with disabilities. But what would it mean in the field of theology?

If all human beings are created in the image and likeness of God, which is what Christian doctrine claims, what does that say about people with disabilities and about God? Can we even talk about God as disabled, as Nancy L. Eiesland did in her book *The Disabled God*? In that book Eiesland, inspired by liberation theology, explores a way to talk about God that enables a transformation within the church for people with disabilities. She claims that no less than a thorough-going transformation of institutional, bureaucratic and theological foundations of the Christian church is essential. Eiesland knows that her way of talking about God cannot represent all people with disabilities, but it is an invitation for both people with disabilities and others who long for emancipatory transformation.

Responding to that invitation to dialogue, I want to question how fruitful the minority group understanding is for a theological interpretation of disability. There are some serious theological questions raised by starting from a specific group's experiences and claiming that this has implications for our understanding of God. The divine by its very nature is a concept that in some way is related to the whole reality. Observe that the group Eiesland starts with is not made up entirely of people with disabilities but of the segment within that group that can identify their experiences with her way of talking about "The Disabled God". This has a parallel in another type of interpretation of disability that starts from the assumption of differences, an interpretation that is quite common, especially in Christian groups. It is an attempt to universalize the experience of disability.

"We all have disabilities" is an expression that is used occasionally. It sounds almost pious and comforting. Almost as if someone were saying to people with disabilities, "You are not so different from other people, so do not make a big deal about the fact that you have a disability." In that respect it sounds as if it started from an assumption that we all have something in common. But I am placing it under the section on difference because I interpret it as a comment that stresses that all human beings live with different forms of limitations. I have serious problems with these kinds of expressions. If all people have disabilities, why do we discuss disability at all? To me this seems more of a defence mechanism denying honest concerns that people have. If we are going to change conditions for people with disabilities, we need to know who we are talking about.

People who want to interpret human life from the assumption of difference have made a valid criticism against the ones who start from the opposite pole, the assumption of likeness. It betrays a lack of sensitivity regarding the dissimilarities among people in this world. All too often white, middle-class, able-bodied men have been set as the standard and the vast majority of persons who do not live in accordance with that standard are seen as exceptions. But how are we to handle this problem in theology? If there is a living God, then we are all connected to that God. If that God is disabled, as Eiesland claims, then everybody has a disabled God. We cannot talk about God without saying something about the world as a whole.

With that in mind, we ask if the minority group model solves the problems that have been identified with the interpretations starting from an assumption of likeness. Those interpretations exclude some people's experiences, yet so do the ones that start from the assumption of difference. The latter do it consciously, something you seldom can say about the former. But even if the problems are identified, and there are no claims that they do not exist, they remain problems. We are left to return to the pole of likeness but to proceed from that starting point with weaker claims.

Likeness with weaker claims

As a pastor, I have talked with many persons either with or without a disability about what they feel disability implies about God and life as a human being in God's world. I have met many reactions. I once read of a person commenting on a text I had written, saying that the writer obviously could not have disability, for no disabled person would use such expressions. "Well, at least one could," I thought.

Sometimes people have become angry with me because I have told them that I am a pastor. They have told me that my disability is in itself proof that there cannot be a God. So my disability, which is seen by some as something that I should thank God for, for others is something that precludes them from Christian faith. With this spectrum of different interpretations one might ask if it is possible to talk about disability at all without hurting someone or offending a group of persons. Should I give up the idea completely, or accept the fact that there always will be someone who does feel hurt when I discuss this complicated matter? Or is there a third alternative? I think there might be, and I want to explore that possibility.

To talk about people with disabilities is to say something about the nature of being human, to expect that in saying "people" we refer to some reality that we all know. In philosophical terms, we may call this ontology. That is to say, we as human beings have some commonalities even if we do not identify them. So we are back to the assumption of human likeness, but we have learned from the criticism we have previously considered. My suggestion is that we change the form of our claims to acknowledge that we may learn something new and so change our opinion. With such an understanding, conflicting interpretations can stand side by side without causing a battle in which one of the interpretations has to be defeated. Conflicting interpretations can stand beside one another and correct each other, and the tension between them may encourage a deepening understanding of the issue. Disability is a human condition and, as such, ambiguous. Allowing multiple interpretations to coexist takes that ambiguity seriously and does not claim a certainty when one cannot be certain.

If we seriously analyzed conflicting interpretations, could we be sure which of them is wrong? In a complex language, each expression has a surplus of meaning; therefore, every interpretation is bound to be wrong in some respect. We will never find one way of understanding disability that is right for every time and every place. As we now look back to different historical interpretations of disability, we hope that people in the future will see our ways of interpreting disability as things of the past. It would be an expression of hubris to believe that we now have come to the end of history and from now on nothing will happen that could possibly change our understanding. I would regard such a claim as quite depressing.

But what would such an attitude mean in practice, in our everyday interaction with human lives, including lives with disability? It would mean that I may not make interpretations that step on other people's freedom to interpret disability for themselves. I can make interpretations from my own perspective, but not in a form that rules out every conflicting interpretation. I cannot claim that anyone who does not share my opinion has misunderstood it completely, or that either of us knows anything for certain. Our interpretations are part of a much larger process through which we slowly grow to a deeper understanding of what life with disability is and can be.

Let us share the one world – a plea for accessibility

Every metaphor becomes problematic if it is pushed too far and as persons we have different feelings towards different metaphors. A metaphor that I personally have problems with is the one that talks about "different worlds", as when someone says that we live in two different worlds, or that to come to one certain place is to discover a new world. I know it is a metaphorical way of emphasizing the differences between contexts. But still I find it problematic because we inhabit only one world. This beautiful blue planet, which I love, is all we've got. We who happen to live in the same time in history have no choice but to share it with one another. That is why I am much happier with the concept of one world. This concept provides a language that we can use to talk about the solidarity that is required in sharing a world, and the problems connected to that.

In regard to disability, the language of one world can be connected to "accessibility". To demand accessibility for people with disabilities is to remind ourselves that we all live in the same world. The question is: How shall we do that? When we talk about accessibility in a confessional Christian setting, we recognize that it has four dimensions; a physical, a social, an ethical and a theological. Let us explore those four dimensions.

The physical dimension is the one I believe most of us are referring to when we talk about accessibility. This dimension is about ramps, accessible restrooms and so on. The international disability symbol is a wheelchair and this seems to indicate that for many persons accessibility for people with disabilities is the same thing as a wheelchair-friendly environment. But accessibility is also about using hearing aid technologies or having good lighting for the visually impaired. When a person in a large gathering says that his or her voice is strong and that you can hear without a microphone or loudspeakers, you can almost be certain that someone is excluded. That sort of behaviour denies accessibility for persons with hearing impairment. Another example of physical accessibility is how we build an environment that is good for persons with different sorts of allergies. We can also think about the form we give to our written information. Is it accessible for persons who are visually impaired? And so we can go on and on, with examples of how we can make our physical environment accessible to people with disabilities.

But this is only one of our four dimensions. Another is the social dimension, how we interact socially with one another. For a long time in my part of the world, families felt guilt and shame for having a family member with a disability. Late in the 20th century adults with mental disabilities were discovered in rural areas of Sweden; the authorities did not know they were there – they had been hidden by their families. With the concept of integration people with disabilities have become people whom we meet in the society. Still there are persons who are not used to meeting persons with disabilities and have an awkward way of handling this new situation. I could tell many funny stories of how I have been treated by persons who meet me for the first time. Let me give you one example.

Once I visited a museum in Stockholm. I asked at the ticket office how much a student entrance fee was. I was holding a twenty krona note in my hand. The lady in the box office pointed at the note and said, "It will cost you more than that." I told her that I understood that and asked her to tell me how much more it would cost. But she gave me the same answer: that it would cost me more than what I held in my hand. So we went on until I saw a sign that said "Students 30 krona", and I asked the lady why she could not tell me that at once. She did not reply.

It is easy to moralize over such behaviour. But moralizing does not help much. It is all right to feel uncertain in new situations, and we do have that right when we experience things for the first time. If someone who never has met a person with cerebral palsy meets me for the first time, I can very well understand that this causes some uncertainty and discomfort. The question is: How do we deal with this uncertainty? If we feel afraid, we can reduce the person we meet to fit our own prejudices. We project our expectations on the persons we meet and never encounter them as themselves. We can also make negative generalizations. If one person with disabilities is one way, every other person is viewed as the same. This is a perceptual mechanism that can make the social environment inaccessible for persons with disabilities.

These are problems that we who live with disabilities meet frequently in our daily life. It causes great frustration. Sometimes we get angry, even if we know that anger does not help much. But one does not have the patience to be a good and informative ambassador for people with disabilities all the time. Sometimes we have to let our frustration out.

The best way to handle these problems is to let persons without disabilities, the temporarily able-bodied, come to know persons with disabilities. We must acknowledge our lack of experience and knowledge, and also admit our curiosity. We must be allowed to put stupid questions. People have asked me the most intimate questions you can imagine, just because they wanted to know: What is it like to live a life with disability? As a person with disability I sometimes get tired of people who claim to be specialists in the field of disability. It is often more enlightening to answer honest questions than to blind the curious with science. People need to acknowledge that reality may be different than they think it is and that they are able to open up their minds to new insights.

The question of accessibility also has an ethical dimension. It is connected to our anthropology, our understanding of what a human being is and what makes human life worth living. This question is connected to the question of autonomy and the right to independence and self-determination. No one is completely independent, and our lives are always influenced by others' decisions. Persons with disabilities are frequently more dependent than others and thus more vulnerable. I remember once I was working in an office when the power failed. All the other employees were frustrated because they had lost the work on their computers, but I remember thinking that if the power did not come back by that afternoon I would not be able to work at all. My colleagues who were able to write with their hands could always use an ordinary pen, but I need a computer to write, or at least an electric typewriter, although there are very few of them still around these days. This example demonstrates a fact that I find hard to deny: As a person with disability, one tends to be more dependent and more vulnerable than others.

This vulnerability poses ethical questions to the whole society. The golden rule, "Whatever you wish that others would do to you, do so to them" (Matt. 7:12), is as always a good rule. Ask yourself how you would like to be handled if you were in the same situation. How would you like assistance to be organized if you needed an assistant for your everyday life? How would you organize your transportation if you could not get a driving licence or use public transportation? What is it that makes a life worth living? Sometimes when I get frustrated over political decisions in the field of disability, I ask myself: "Would politicians like to have their lives organized in the way persons with disabilities have to organize theirs due to the political decisions those same politicians make?"

In Christian settings, the question of accessibility has to be considered in a particular dimension – the theological one. If we understand disability as a human condition as one part of humanity's common experience of what it is to be a human being in God's world, then this understanding will have implications for our theological anthropology. A different theological anthropology may change our understanding of God, leading us to formulate a new theology. What does it say about God that God creates a world where life with disability is a possibility? Have the biblical stories about healing miracles any implications for our understanding of disability in God's world? These and many additional hard theological questions are raised by disability, and we cannot build up a fully accessible environment within our churches unless we deal with them theologically.

I have mentioned four dimensions of accessibility, the physical, attitudinal, ethical and theological. All of these are interconnected. We cannot deal with one dimension without dealing with the other three. The way we design our physical facilities has implications for our attitudes, and is also an ethical question. How we deal with ethical questions yields theological implications. If our churches are to become communities that are fully open and inclusive for people with disabilities, our approach to accessibility must take all of the four dimensions into account.

As a person with disability I want to turn to every part of human society and God's church and urge them: Let us share your world! Because your world is also my world and every person's world, and because, so far, this is the only world there is.

Let us together tear down every barrier that prevents the full participation in our churches of persons with or without disabilities. Let us acknowledge our mutual interdependence. If we live in the same world, we are dependent on each other. Anyone can acquire a disability at any point in life, so to advocate for accessibility for people with disabilities is to ask for a society where everyone can feel safe and secure. Even those who lack a disability are dependent on society in various ways. We live in a society where independence is the ideal; independence is and indeed ought to be an important concept for the struggle towards liberation on the part of people with disabilities. But we can still recognize the fact that every person is dependent regardless of disability. This general dependence that is a part of human life simply becomes more apparent in a life with disability. To live in a society where it is acceptable to acknowledge one's own dependence is to be part of a society where we all can feel safe. Every person is weak, and therefore dependent, in some circumstances.

But to share a world is also to share the fact that we interpret things differently. What some interpret as a cross, others interpret as a crown. We have to accept that and live with that. We need to find ways in which different and conflicting interpretations are allowed to exist without excluding each other but instead functioning to challenge, correct and enrich each other. To share a world is to acknowledge that no interpretation has the complete truth, and that even when some interpretations are in conflict with each other they each can have valuable insights, so that we do not necessarily have to choose between them. To share a world is to acknowledge that our knowledge is imperfect and therefore needs improvement. We will never reach complete knowledge, at least not in this world, so let us share our interpretations and walk together on the road towards a deeper understanding.

Living with Disability

Samuel Kabue

Following the section on hermeneutics by Arne Fritzson, this second part of our book reflects my experience both as an African with a disability and as someone in disability work with the churches. As I have considered Arne's piece, I have been struck by our commonalities and differences. Arne and I are both people with disabilities. We are frequently classified by this title in a common category. We might talk of common experiences in the way society's attitudes subject us to discriminatory practices, whether inadvertently or out of prejudice or ignorance. However, in our individual situations there is very little in common between us. He says about himself, "I am a person with a disability, cerebral palsy, and I am a Christian, an ordained pastor in a small, reformed Swedish free church, the Mission Covenant Church of Sweden. I am also a male, married, Western, academically trained, white person with a middle-class background." Reviewing this list of what he is, I am all the more convinced of the great difference between him and me. There are more characteristics of his which will never be attributed to me. It is obvious that we are each products of our history and our social environment. We are from very different backgrounds. Our disabilities too are very different.

The recent World Council of Churches' interim statement on disabilities entitled "A Church of All and for All" notes that persons with disabilities have diverse attributes and individual characteristics. Various disabilities cause physical pain and/or a shortened life span. Some of us have physical and/or mental impairments that date from birth or early childhood. We have come to terms with our disabilities by diverse routes. We come from a variety of cultures and are thus culturally conditioned just like everyone else. Some are fortunate to have been supported by the loving bonds of family, friends, church, community and different disability cultures and groups, while others have had to struggle alone. Some of us have been comforted and sustained by our faith in a loving God.

The statement rightly notes that what most disabled people around the world do share in common is the experience of being discriminated against. We have been marginalized by patronizing and paternalistic attitudes, made the objects of ridicule and fear, or just ignored and left out. The negative view society has and the stigma associated with disability make people with disabilities vulnerable to the manipulations of those who promote easy commercial cures or the religious zealots who offer miraculous healing in an atmosphere of superficial friendship.

Arne states, "Now, when the World Council of Churches provides a space for this important conversation, why should I occupy that space? I, who belong to a culture of colonizers, even though my country had a very small part in the history of European colonization?" I am reawakened by these sentiments to the fact that I am blind, from a country in the South where people with disabilities receive no state personal maintenance support whatsoever, where devices to assist people with disabilities are very rare as there is no organized support other than what the family or the individual can afford, and I have been the subject of a colonial legacy. I, too, have a story to tell.

I met Arne five years ago during the eighth assembly of the World Council of Churches at Harare, Zimbabwe. Before that, we had been corresponding over a period of two years in preparation for our participation in that assembly as disability advisers. The one thing that I knew about Arne over these years was that he was a person with a disability. This was the main thing that bonded us together in our preparation. There were two things that I came to know about Arne when I met him personally. First, something that we often joke about now, is that I learned that Arne was a man only on meeting him. For some reason, possibly the name, I had always assumed that I had been corresponding with a woman. On telling him this, he jokingly retorted, "Are you disappointed?"

The second thing I discovered was his disability. I had never bothered to find out what his disability was. Although I had serious difficulties understanding him during our encounter in Harare because of his speech impairment, I already had read many good ideas in his correspondence, so

I was anxious to hear more directly from him as a person. I therefore had a driving ambition to understand him. As I think of this today, I wonder how many people, especially in the social environment that I come from, would have the patience to listen to someone with a speech impairment such as Arne's unless they had some background experience as I did. Perhaps this may explain why there is no visible evidence of such people in the interactive social circles in my country. I do not know of any person with Arne's degree of speech impairment in my country in the academic field or the church's ordained ministry. I have been asking myself where such people, who have above-average intellect and would have excelled as gospel ministers or academics, end up. It is most likely that parents do not see the need to take such children to school and, if they did, our teachers would dismiss them at the childhood stage as uneducable. Many must have been denied the opportunities which would have propelled them to prominence.

Let it be understood that lack of opportunities is not limited to people with impaired speech alone. Recent statistics released by the Kenya society for the blind indicated that there are about 160,000 people with visual impairment in Kenya. Only 2 percent of these are in any form of gainful employment. One may rightly wonder what happens to the 98 percent of men, women, youth and children with visual impairment in a country where there is no form of social security or income maintenance support, unlike in the developed countries.

The disparity between developed and underdeveloped nations reminds me of an encounter with a woman with a disability during a visit I made to England a few years ago. We were sharing our experiences of the frustrations we go through in our day-to-day lives as people with disabilities. As I listened to her, I could not help thinking that some of the issues people in the North consider to be part of their struggles may not make sense to us in the South.

This lady told me of a programme called Meals on Wheels. The programme supplies meals to people with severe disabilities in their homes, free of charge. My friend's problem is that the meal never arrives in time. It is brought either too early or too late and this is a major problem in so far as she was concerned. It struck her as an infringement of the right of the recipients to eat at the right time. As I thought about the situation in my country, my reaction to this complaint may not have pleased her. I said to her that in my country, it would not matter whether the meal was brought in the middle of the night or at any hour, it would still be most welcome. Many of our disabled people go for days without any meal, and even when they get it, it is hardly what would be called a meal. When you hear that people are dying of hunger in parts of Africa, people with disabilities will have died long before that.

It has already been pointed out that, disabled or not, we are a product of our history and our social experience. Like anybody else, there are many distinct events that have uniquely shaped my life, first as a Kenyan and secondly as a person with a disability. I was born when Kenya was still a British colony struggling for independence. This was a very difficult time, as the country was in a state of emergency owing to the seven years of armed struggle mounted by the Kenyans against British colonial forces. I came from one of the most affected parts, central Kenya. It was a time of utter poverty and hunger, as people had no time to concentrate on their economic mainstay because of the war. Although I went to school when this situation had eased at the end of the armed struggle, my life is still marked by it. Besides the effects of poverty, one other effect of the war was that, like many other children my age, I began school two years late. This remained a constant reminder of the colonial experience throughout my school life. As a child I joined daily in singing the British anthem, "God Save the Queen", in my local language. This I did for nearly four years from the start of my school life to the time Kenya became independent at the end of 1963. Thus, when Arne says that he is from a culture of colonizers, I can talk of colonial experience at the personal level.

I lost my sight at the age of sixteen just after entering high school. This came four years after our national independence. Doctors explained my condition as detachment of the retina. My only encounter with any blind person at the time had been from a distance and involved only old people. Loss of sight came as the most devastating blow to me. I was a young person hoping to become someone important in a country that was rapidly changing. I just could not accept it when doctors pronounced me blind and insisted that my only hope for education would be to start life anew in a school for the blind. My understanding was that this meant starting all over and doing another eight years before returning to the educational level where I already was. This was something I could not endure, and I did all I could to resist even the idea of being taken to find out what I needed in order to be admitted to the school. I was prevailed upon through patient persuasion, and it was only after an interview with the head teacher at the Salvation Army school for the blind that I learned that all I needed was to learn Braille and then continue on at the level I had left before losing my sight. This was another stage in my life that called for a different socialization and reorientation.

Having grown up under the care of a Christian mother and having attended a Presbyterian school, I was already grounded in the Christian faith by the time I lost my sight. All the same, I could not for a long time help wondering why God would allow such a thing in my life. I was very doubtful at one stage about my Christian faith and the existence of God. One thing that helped me to recollect my faith and that uplifted me was my experience at the school for the blind.

My initial encounter with my new life was at the primary school. This Salvation Army institution had begun as a rehabilitation centre for the war-blinded soldiers returning from the second world war. Only later did it admit young people for academic education. I arrived there to begin my Braille lessons on Tuesday, 17 September 1968. It was the tradition of the then twenty-two-year-old mission school to conduct a mid-week service at the chapel every Wednesday. Still hurting from the frustrations of my first two days in this new environment, I was ushered into the chapel for my very first worship at the school. I felt most welcome but, above all, very impressed by the cheers and melodious singing from children, some very young and others nearly as old as myself, if not older. The joy that filled the chapel was a major challenge to me, especially as it occurred to me that many of these students had never been able to see as I had. Yet their voices were full of praise and joy. This was a turning point in my faith and life as a Christian. The days that followed revealed to me that these children were little concerned by the fact that they did not see. They joked, played and laughed as though they were no different from any other children I had known. I became very determined to do what needed to be done, even to learn Braille, to get on with my education without having to sorrow over my loss of sight. Yes, this was another beginning for me.

The church had established a high school next to the primary school just a year before. This was the right place for me to be, but I could not be admitted there initially because I had to learn Braille at the primary school and be assessed as to whether I could cope. The assessment included how quickly I could learn Braille and adapt to my new life. Admission to the high school was very competitive as it was the only such school in the whole of East Africa. It was made clear that my acceptance to a high school class was dependent on mastering the Braille code within the three months prior to the new year. This goal called for a lot of determination. An individualized programme to learn Braille was organized and a very effective instructor attached to me. The teaching sessions took place in a corner of the library. By the time the school closed for Christmas holidays, about two and a half months following my arrival, I had managed to learn the entire code and what was left was for me to practise reading fast as I got ready to get back to the classroom in the new year. I went home for my holidays armed with several Braille books. Among these was a copy of the gospel according to

Saint Mark. This I read several times through in the one-month period before going back to school.

The language of loss

No matter how quickly I adjusted to my blindness, the language of "loss" kept on ringing in my ears as perpetrated by family members, relatives' friends and the wider community. I kept being reminded that a tragedy had happened in my life through the pity shown to me. Pity has the dynamic that the one to whom it is shown is considered not only in a worse situation than the one who shows pity, but also is considered inferior. This dynamic was evident in the many things people said I could no longer do even as they offered to do them for me. In many cases their assumptions were wrong, as they did not appreciate the adjustments and the training that I was going through. Life was less bearable during my holidays when I met people I had known before and whose faces and figures were still fresh in my memory but who wanted to treat me differently than before. Worse still, meeting new people whose faces and figures I had never experienced was one of the greatest reminders of my blindness and the loss that I had to bear. These new people had no faces so far as I was concerned, and it was impossible to make correct judgments or imagine how they looked. Thinking about this often convinced me of my "loss".

The greatest struggle experienced by people with disabilities today has to do with perceived loss. Although the idea of loss may be associated more with people who become adventitiously disabled, as was the case with me, even those whose disabilities are congenital are not free from it. Where the idea of "loss" is played down, it tends to be replaced by the even more negative idea of deficiency. This presumption of deficiency has, throughout the history of mankind, brought about barriers in the way persons with disabilities relate with the rest of society.

In the early days of human history when we lived by hunting and gathering, there was truly no place for people who were not able to engage in this livelihood. One had to be strong and able to hunt or get into the forest to collect roots and fruits to eat. It was truly survival of the fittest. People with disabilities could not survive in those conditions. The emphasis on maintaining a "fit" body continued, with differing degrees from society to society. Among the Greek city-states of Athens and Sparta, everybody in the society had to be a soldier. So far as these societies were concerned, a healthy mind deserved a healthy body. Without a "healthy" body that could allow one to become a soldier, a male was considered unfit as a citizen. Such people were abandoned and had very little chance of surviving. Of course, there were exemptions on rare occasions; a person with disabilities might have other qualities that made him acceptable, though only in the face of a lot of resistance.

Tolerance for the existence of persons with disabilities began with the agrarian revolution when surplus food was available for those unable to engage actively in the production. Some people with disabilities were brought up on large farms where they were allowed to survive and do the little that was within their abilities. However, a large majority of them were still ignored and lived in appalling conditions. Organized care began with the rise of religious orders in the middle ages. Initially, they were cared for in monasteries and convent infirmaries. This was largely influenced by the idea of a merciful and caring God who demanded or expected the same virtues from the people of God. This care largely involved looking after the physical and material needs of these people without having to get them actively involved in productive work. In most cases, even their spiritual welfare was not a concern. This type of care led to the rise of professional carers who were expected to know much about the needs of the people they cared for and, for this reason, to speak on their behalf. There also arose a need to raise resources for this work elsewhere, thus perfecting caring as a career. This is what led to the culture of charity, which is anathema to modern disability advocates.

Yet it is against this background that the learning institutions that pioneered education for persons with disabilities later grew. They were largely charitable organizations either owned by the churches or with very close association to churches and mission societies. In most parts of Africa, where these developments are much more recent, these institutions were part of the missionary work and the way funds were raised to sustain them took a charity-oriented approach which did not play a very positive role in the attitudes instilled in the students. On joining the school for the blind, this was one of the negative things that I noted and which I have continued to address in my disability advocacy.

Let me take the case of the Salvation Army high school for the blind as an example. As noted before, this institution was unique in the entire region. Therefore, it attracted visitors from far and wide. As these visitors were taken around, the only language you heard was that of "helping". Even the most junior cook or cleaner always said, "We are helping these children." This obviously perpetuated the notion of deficiency. It was not a language of building.

Two questions kept coming to my mind as I reflected years later on this language from the staff of the school. In the first place, I asked myself what difference it made for these cooks if they worked in a school for the blind or any other school. At the end of the month, they expected their pay, as they would from any other employment. Why then the language of "helping"? The other thing that troubled me was the attitude instilled in the students as they heard this language throughout their school life. They had to grow up as people who saw themselves marked by a permanent deficiency and who must as a result be always on the receiving end, people to be helped at all times. Some even developed the attitude that they would always have to be objects of aid on the account of their blindness. This trait was still evident later as I observed people who stayed for many years in these residential institutions. This is why I grew to advocate an integrated educational system for persons with disabilities wherever this is practical.

The interpretation of human life, abilities and deficiencies have tended to be seen in terms of historical contexts in which people have formulated interpretations. It may help to look at our contemporary period and the opportunities that are available to us. Theology too needs to be flexible and to contexualize our understanding of disability. At the time of Jesus, it was theologically correct to argue that when making a feast, one should invite those with disabilities because they would not be able to invite others in turn. In today's world there is a struggle for appropriate equalization of opportunities and living environments for all, including persons with disabilities. Because they are self-sufficient, persons with disabilities do not have any reason not to organize feasts and invite others. It is in the light of this that the current WCC interim theological statement, "A Church of All and for All", raises the fundamental observation that the language of "loss" is inadequate in characterizing disability, and we would do better to think in terms of "plurality". Perhaps disability is something that God has created in order to build a plural, more diverse and richer world.

Sin, forgiveness and healing

Another facet of the phenomenon of disability has to do with its association with sin, and therefore with forgiveness and healing. This association has its roots in the religious beliefs of different societies at different stages of their history. The underlying idea is that disability occurs as a result of sins or misdeeds of either the person concerned or other people related to him or her. This idea comes with belief in a vengeful God who will take away something from a person as punishment for unacceptable action or behaviour. Judaeo-Christian culture itself has not been spared this superstition. This can be seen in St John's gospel, 9:1-3, where the disciples of the Lord Jesus confront him on meeting a man who was blind since birth. Their question to their Master was, "Who sinned, this man or his parents, that he was born blind?" Jesus exonerated both the man and his parents by answering, "Neither has this man sinned nor his parents: but that the works of God should be made manifest in him."

The Master's answer has taken a very long time to be internalized into the theology of the Christian faith. Today, some Christian churches, especially in Africa, still preach that disabilities are a result of works of the devil. The presence of people with disabilities in such churches is viewed as a failure by the church to combat the devil. It is therefore seen as a challenge to the church that calls for constantly invoking Christ's power to heal, and when this does not happen the concerned person with disability is blamed for lack of faith. This is the surest way of telling the person that he or she does not belong. It can be said to be a major factor why many persons with disabilities have kept to themselves, away from the church.

Most people with disabilities will have personal examples of the discouragements that come with the message of physical healing. Such promises are promoted by people who truly believe, though wrongly, that God's intervention is always to be called upon when the church comes into contact with a person with a disability. Two of many examples from my experience are of particular interest in that they occurred early in the years of my blindness.

The most dramatic incident was when I was in third form, in my middle teens. One Sunday afternoon I crossed the town with two friends, David and Bernard, journeying to the shops around the market where we could buy postal stamps. Bernard had substantial residual vision, so he acted as a sighted guide for David and me, as both of us were totally blind.

We had just bought our stamps and were on our way back to school when we met a woman preaching at the market gate. We had no idea what she was preaching about, but it may have had something to do with divine healing. We had no intention of listening to her, but some people intercepted us and pleaded with us to have the woman pray for us to recover our sight. We were prevailed upon and we found ourselves kneeling before the woman. After the prayer, the woman declared that we had received our sight back. Every-body rushed around us, and for a time I thought my friends may have received their sight and that I was the only one left blind. People started placing all sorts of items such as pota-toes, pineapples, bananas and sugar canes in front of us and asking us what they were. My friend Bernard kept shouting what these were, yet since they were being brought rather close to our eyes and David like me was not responding, I knew that he could still not see and that Bernard was just using the little sight we all three knew he had. Every time he responded, there was pandemonium – shouts and ecstasy that made the crowd continue to swell. Although Bernard may have been under the delusion that he could see better than before, I must say I was personally very irritated at his response because the more he named objects, the louder the shouts of excitement became. The crowd was getting bigger, with nearly the whole market coming to witness the healing, making it impossible for us to move.

A police car on patrol came by and the policemen in it wanted to find out what was happening. They had seen us struggling to get out of the crowd that was shouting with excitement. They approached us and asked us whether it was true that we could see. I promptly said no, and David sup-ported me. The policemen cleared the way for us by scatter-ing the crowd, but before we had walked a few metres with Bernard holding our hands to guide us, the crowd had again built up and we could not move. The policemen could not control the joyful mob. They decided that the best thing was to put us in their car and take us back to school, and this was to me a great relief. They dropped us right in the school and we rushed to the dining hall, as it was already suppertime. I personally was feeling very embarrassed and did not talk to anyone about what had happened. I ate my meal very quickly and went straight to my room and closed myself in.

After just a few minutes, there was a commotion in the school. A good section of the crowd from the market had fol-lowed us to the school, and since word had quickly spread around, students from the neighbouring schools had joined the crowd, making it very big. I could hear the voices of some girls from the neighbouring high school Christian union outside my dormitory but I could not bring myself to open the door to talk to them. Like me, my friends David and Bernard had gone to their rooms and had decided not to identify themselves with what was happening. The teacher on duty could not manage to deal with the crowd that was demanding to see the three boys who had been healed. He reported the matter to the headmaster who called the police to help get the crowd out of the school. It took a long time for us to disclose what had happened to us, as we did not know how the school administration would respond to the matter.

The second incident that I would like to cite took place a little later in the same year. I had just been elected the secretary of the Christian union in my school. We had very good working relations with the Christian union in the immediately neighbouring school. As the secretary, I was the main liaison between the two Christian unions. There was one particular girl in this other school whom I had come to know through Christian union interactions, and we eventually came to be quite close. Mercy was her name. She was spiritual, open and very courageous in speaking to any person, including teachers whom she met. She attended our school's evening Sunday services in the chapel occasionally and always presented a song. She became well-known to everybody in the school including the headmaster.

Some time during that year, an international evangelist named Maurice Cerulo was visiting Kenya and organizing crusades in Nairobi (crusades are open-air evangelistic gatherings). Mercy had attended one of these crusades and so was convinced that I should attend. Although she was not explicit with me as to all the reasons why she wanted me to go with her, she believed that this evangelist had the gift of healing and that I could receive healing through him. I could see her deep concern and conviction on this matter, but I had two problems. First, I could not understand how I could attend a crusade on a weekday in Nairobi, forty kilometres away from my school, and especially in the evening. Secondly, I had already become disillusioned with miracle healings from my own past experience and from stories I had heard from friends in the school. I respected Mercy so much that I could not be quite open with her and tell her that I was actually not interested. I simply told her that the school would not allow me to go. That was what I believed, and I thought that this would also deter her. Without even consulting me, she decided to approach my headmaster, Captain Michael Rich, for permission. Miraculously and I cannot tell how, she secured his permission. As I later learned, she had pledged to him that she would take me from the school and that she would herself bring me back to school.

It was on a Wednesday that we left Thika for Nairobi at four-thirty in the afternoon. Mercy was with several friends, girls and boys from her school, most of whom I already knew. We discussed nothing about the possibility of my healing on the way. This made me quite comfortable, as I had been afraid that this could come up in our discussion. I knew Mercy to be a very open girl. We were at Kamukunji Grounds, where the crusade was taking place in Nairobi, at six. We found the evangelist already preaching. After the sermon, there was an altar call as well as a prayer call for those who needed healing. We were not called to the front as is usual with such crusades. Maybe this was because it was already late and getting quite dark. We were prayed for wherever we happened to be. Mercy, without a word to me, held my eyes and prayed along as the evangelist prayed. But after praying, she did not ask me if I had regained my sight. At the end of the prayers, we gathered together in our small group that had come from Thika, went to the bus stop and took a bus back to Thika. I could not help imagining the expectations of the group as we all moved in silence. It seemed to me that my being persuaded to attend that meeting was something that had been discussed and there were a lot of expectations that my going would result in a miraculous healing. Going back the same way I had come seemed likely to be a disappointment to the group.

True to her word, Mercy and her friends made sure that I was back at school by eleven o'clock. I returned to the room which I shared with three other boys, who were still awake and waiting for me. I narrated to them the whole story of how Mercy had obtained permission from the headmaster, and this surprised them as much as it had surprised me. One positive thing about this incident was that although I did not receive healing, this did not shake my relationship with Mercy. She also did not put me through such an experience again and did not openly condemn me for lack of faith, an experience other persons with disabilities have had to go through.

In extreme cases, emphasis on physical healing has sown confusion to the detriment of the Christian faith. There have been incidents in which preachers of the gospel seemed to be seeking their own glory, making themselves look like liars and making the gospel appear ridiculous. One illustration here will do. A few years ago, a certain popular Western evangelist who regularly visits my country organized a very well attended crusade at our coastal town of Mombasa. Advertisements for the crusade with messages that the sick and the disabled would be prayed for had earlier been placed all over. On the promised day, children from a school for the physically handicapped in the town were brought specifically to experience healing. After a very moving sermon, the evangelist requested that all those with healing needs be brought forward for prayers, and the ushers enthusiastically collected these children together. After the prayer the evangelist declared that everybody had been healed and authoritatively ordered those still on their crutches to throw them away and run towards him. Those in wheelchairs were also ordered to jump out of them and run towards him. A group of the children obeyed these orders literally and in their attempt to run towards the preacher, many of them fell and either broke their residual limbs or received very bad bruises. In the commotion that ensued, some lost crutches that they still needed.

As could be expected, this news hit the headlines and there was a serious outcry against the evangelist. A friend of mine who was at the time the head of the physiotherapy department at the medical training centre in Nairobi approached me as a leader in the disability movement and also in my capacity as the staff member responsible for a disability programme in a church organization. He requested that I join a legal suit against the evangelist. The charge was that of misleading children with disabilities and thus causing bodily harm to them. His argument was that even if there was nothing that could have been done about the harm already caused, the man should be restrained from presenting such misleading messages in future. Although I certainly did not condone what had taken place I also did not, as a person working within a church organization, want to participate in such an endeavour. All the same, I kept wondering what the church needs to do to avoid situations like these that discredit the Christian ministry.

Although I have no doubt God can heal, I believe that this happens within the scope of God's own will and timing and, even then, does not happen to everyone. Nor does it require great preachers to come all the way from Europe or America to Africa for God to carry out plans for healing. As seen from the examples above, emphasis on physical healing has at times worked very negatively on the faith of persons with disabilities. Many have felt it embarrassing to attend worship or crusades by the so-called great world evangelists because, when they do so, the ushers in such events cannot conceive the idea of one going to such an event purely for spiritual blessings and nourishment. They always assume that you have gone there for physical healing and will often coerce you to go to the front for divine healing prayers. If no healing takes place, one is presumed to have no faith and is told no less than that.

These experiences in Christian crusades that put their emphasis on faith healing is something that I myself have gone through, and I can bear witness to the feeling that comes to one when such a thing happens. I can weather it today, but it was much more difficult in those early days of my blindness. I have grown to understand the gospel and to know that God has ways of dealing with us that are very different from human understanding. In this respect, I am reminded of St Paul the apostle who, though he had performed many miracles ranging from healing to raising the dead, lived with a problem which he refers to in 2 Corinthians 12:7-9 as a thorn in the flesh. He testified that he pleaded with God about this three times, but God's answer to him was, "My grace is sufficient for you." My understanding of this is that our physical conditions should never be grounds to make us not carry out the mission God appoints us to fulfil. God will accompany us and give us the necessary grace to handle all the situations we encounter.

The WCC interim theological statement "A Church of All and for All" provides some insights into alternative ways to view the subject of healing and disabilities in the modern age. The healing section differentiates between healing and cure; the gospel healing stories are seen not merely as restoration of the body but more as the individual's restoration in and into the society. It is an act of recognizing previously outcast people as human and joining them to the rest of the community in their day-to-day occupations. When the blind Bartimeus's sight is restored, he immediately joins in the procession with all the others. When the crippled man at the Beautiful Gate has his ability restored, he joins other worshippers in the temple, something he had never done before. He is accepted as one of them and is no longer a stranger. The cardinal message here is that when we create an inviting environment and provide space for full participation and active involvement of people with disabilities in the church's life, we are participating in Christ's healing ministry.

Effects of social attitudes

It took me a few years to realize that living with my blindness was neither a tragedy nor a problem for my day-to-day life. What was a problem was the constant reminder from those around me that I live with a disability. The major problems for persons with disabilities are the social attitudes and barriers imposed on them by society. These come either in the form of unrealistic expectations or unfounded imaginings of what disability does to one's personality, character and ability. It is difficult for those who think that either wearing a blindfold or living in darkness is the same as living with blindness to imagine how people can be blind and be happy, let alone do things for themselves. This is made worse by the isolation in which most people with disabilities find themselves, especially when they are educated and trained in residential disability institutions that make them strangers to the society in which they belong. It is only through acceptance, integration and active involvement that people with disabilities come to be fully understood in terms of their capacities and possible contributions to society.

I am reminded of the very different experiences I and a friend of mine, who is blind like me, went through after our graduation from the university of Nairobi as teachers. At that time, graduating teachers were automatically posted to teach in public schools wherever there were vacancies. Principals of well-to-do national schools would be allowed to see the list of graduating teachers and their grades in order to influence the posting of the brightest teachers to their schools. Fortunately or unfortunately, such a list would have only the name and the grades but not other circumstances or characteristics of the graduating teacher. My friend happened to have been picked by a principal on the basis of his grades. On reporting to the school, the principal rejected him on discovering that he was blind. He insisted that his was not a school for the blind. To him, a blind person could only teach in a school for the blind. The posting authorities stood their ground, insisting that my friend who had been picked on merit had to remain and teach in that school. Of course, this was a very bad beginning to anyone's career, but it was also a challenge to my friend to prove to the principal that he could teach. It took three months to convince the principal that he was worthy of a posting in his school.

On the other hand, I was posted to a large high school where on arrival I received a rousing welcome from the principal. I was assigned duties immediately in several classes. The allocation of the teaching load struck other teachers in the school as unkind since it was like that of any other teacher in the school. They expected that the principal should have been "kind", giving me a light load because I was blind. However, to me my assignment was an expression of confidence in me as a teacher like any other, and the challenge for me was to prove that I was worthy of being a teacher. It was much later that I came to learn why the principal had so much confidence in me from the very start, even when he did not know me. On sharing with him, I came to learn that he had a classmate in college who was blind. The principal had become convinced that blindness was not a factor in one's success, provided that the social environment was right. Although this was very positive and as such very encouraging for me, unrealistic expectations at the other extreme could play out negatively. For instance, integration should not be seen as merely thrusting a person with a disability into the deep end without the necessary support systems.

Even with all necessary support systems, problems may arise when a person with a disability is valued purely on the basis of his or her disability as viewed by those around him or her. The church has done just this at times, partly in self-justification for having put in place certain affirmative structures specific to persons with disabilities. Unfortunately, these institutions, though well intentioned, have led to the isolation of persons with disabilities. Consequently, the church has tended to take too long to discover the full potential of persons with disabilities. As a result of isolation, however well-meaning, walls are erected.

On first completing my university entrance examination, my desire had been to pursue a career as an ordained minister. The procedure in my Presbyterian church demanded that this process begin with approval by my local congregation, which would in turn recommend me to the parish board. As required, I made my application with great hope that it would be passed on accordingly. It never went beyond the local church level, and nobody gave me any explanation as to what had happened. Little did I realize that my blindness and the years of my absence while in the residential school had made me a stranger to my congregation. It was clear that the local church committee had a problem with me, but they were not willing either to disclose what it was or to discuss it with me. As I later learned, they could not recommend me, as they felt that they could not stand surety for either my eligibility or suitability to serve in the ministry.

This came about despite the fact that the congregation was where I had been baptized as a child, attended Sunday school and even after the onset of my blindness served both as a member of the youth group and a Sunday school teacher during my school holidays. Moreover, my academic level and achievements were not in question so far as admission to the theological college was concerned. I could not imagine any reason that stood in my way other than blindness alone.

Frustrated by the lack of response, I decided to approach the matter at the Presbyterian church's head office. I met the church general secretary of that time who promised to make some intervention, but from the encounters that followed it became clear that there was no commitment on his part. We had several meetings with him, yet it did not seem as though this matter ever moved beyond his desk. Then I thought of approaching the secretary to the training committee, a Scottish missionary church minister. He too could not understand fully this behaviour from all those I had approached and, although he did not say it, he too saw my blindness as a mitigating factor. He advised that it could take a rather long time to go through the necessary processes for church approval, and I should not lose any other opportunity that would come my way. I informed him that by then I had already received admission at the university of Nairobi for a bachelor of education degree, and he felt that I could still pursue my ambition to serve the church even after my first degree. That is the route that I followed, but even after completing my first degree and securing a job as a teacher, I still wanted to join the ordained ministry. I approached Christoffel Blindenmission, an Austrian Christian organization in disability work.

They were willing to give me a scholarship but only on the condition that my church would sign to recommend me and promise that they would give me an opportunity to serve as a minister following the completion of my studies. The church was not willing to commit itself, and so I again lost an opportunity.

After twelve years in government service in different capacities, I found myself working for the National Council of Churches of Kenya (NCCK). Though not an ordained minister, I was all the same in the Christian ministry, in a position that gave me much-needed interaction with the churches and hence a lot of awareness. It happened that the NCCK, which was undergoing a major re-evaluation of its Christian witness and services, had decided to establish a desk on persons with disabilities. Being aware of the World Council of Churches (WCC) and its work on disabilities, the NCCK intended to have a programme that would challenge the churches to work towards inclusion of persons with disabilities in their witness and service. A conference, their very first on disability, had recommended that the desk be staffed by a person with a disability.

On returning from further studies in England where I had gone on a WCC scholarship awarded through the NCCK, I was informed by a senior staff member that the council was looking for a person to establish this work and that he thought I could do it. He advised me to make an appointment with the general secretary to discuss the possibility. The general secretary, who was no stranger to me as he knew me well through interviews for the scholarship and other previous interactions, informed me that he had been looking for a person like me and that he would organize an interview panel to find out whether I was suitable. This was organized within two days and, after the interview, the general secretary informed me that he wanted me to take up the job immediately.

Working with the NCCK at senior staff level gave me a lot of exposure and experience in aspects of its work. After five years in disability work, I was promoted to head the entire advocacy work of the council which included governance, economic justice, human rights, family life education, peace and reconciliation, disability and gender. This gave me even greater interaction with all the heads of member churches of the council. I also had many staff under me none of whom was a person with a disability. Never was my blindness an issue as we worked together, and this proves that what persons with disabilities need is equalization of opportunities in all areas so that they may discover what they can or cannot do. I remember once having a discussion with an elderly church leader who was the secretary to the Presbyterian church's training committee when I was seeking to get into training for ministry after my first degree. I reminded him that the church leaders had blocked my path towards an ordained ministry, but he simply dismissed this by retorting, "What you are doing is even more important than being in the ordained ministry." Looking at my church today, 25 years since I made my unsuccessful effort to train for the ministry, I wonder whether anything has changed. I do not know of any blind Presbyterian minister in the country, and I cannot believe that there has not been anybody interested. This is probably a sign of walls yet to be dismantled. Doors remain shut by social attitudes.

Another aspect of unhelpful attitudes in the church is the tendency to be evasive either out of laziness, ignorance or simple neglect. This is often characterized by seeking the easy way out. A few years ago, a deaf friend of mine narrated an incident that he considered to have had a very great influence in his life and especially his Christian ministry. This took place when he was a student in a residential mission vocational rehabilitation centre. He attended a Sunday service at a church close to the centre one morning and felt that he had not participated as he could not hear what the priest was saying. He decided to approach the priest after the service to explain to him that he could not follow the service, in the hope that they together could work out some solution. On explaining to the priest why he had decided to speak with him, the priest without any hesitation responded, "God knows that you are deaf." To my friend, and for that matter to anyone, this answer does raise certain fundamental questions. In the first place, was my friend in the right place? Was he expected to attend a worship service? Would he have the courage to attend a service again? All in all, what did the priest mean by this all too obvious statement that God knew that my friend was deaf? It is incidents like this, and they are not so few in the experience of would-be worshippers with disabilities, which have kept people away from houses of worship and thus excluded from making their contribution to the church.

Fortunately, my friend was a man of greater will and determination than the average person with disability. Today, he is involved in a full-time ministry to the deaf. To him, the answer he received from the priest many years ago has remained a motivating factor behind what he does. However, it is necessary for the church to address what has resulted from the neglect of the deaf in its ministry. Today we have many exclusive churches for the deaf like the ones my friend has been involved in founding and through which he ministers. The reason for this trend can be explained by the kind of answer my friend received many years ago.

In this day and age of sign language communication and other means of technology to facilitate communication with the deaf, do we still need situations where the deaf worship on their own in isolation from other worshippers? Some will say that this is all right since among the deaf there are those who see themselves as a linguistic group rather than considering deafness as a disability. However, whether we see the deaf as a linguistic group or as people with disability, there is need for their fellowship with other Christians and their being able to contribute to enriching the lives of others. We in churches have failed in our effort towards this ideal. Our failure has been a result of the inability to accommodate one another either due to our ignorance, fear of taking up responsibility, or failure to appreciate that we all have gifts without which the church of Christ is not complete.

The failure to understand disability and its real effects on the daily lives of people affects not only our lives in the church but also general social life. This is evident in people around us, including those in the church, discouraging participation even in what seem very ordinary and normal activities. Let me illustrate this again with a personal experience. Weddings in my part of the world are big social events. I wanted mine to be no different and so went ahead and printed invitation cards which were circulated among friends and relatives alike. There was one man whom I had known for a very long time and whom I thought I should invite. He had been a member of my church from when I was very young. I had very fond memories of him. My earliest such recollection was of an occasion when, as a very young Sunday school child, I was run over by a cyclist on my way home. The man was on his way to church and nearby when this happened. The cyclist wanted to run away, but the man intercepted him. The most memorable thing was that he took time to ensure that he got me to my mother immediately, and she took me for treatment of my bruises.

While I was growing up, this man ran the only bookshop in my home town and this made him seem one of the very enlightened personalities around. As a growing child, I very much admired him. I frequented his shop either to buy a book or just to see what he had on display. I did for a time lose touch with him on going to boarding school after the onset of my blindness but after some years, during my senior high school days, I began again to visit the bookshop with friends but this time always with someone guiding me. The man was no stranger to me, and this is why I thought that I would invite him to my wedding.

Accompanied by a friend, I visited the man armed with an invitation card. With all the excitement of anybody who would have been in my position at the time, I presented him with the card. I was very embarrassed by his reaction. He kept quiet for a while and then said to me, "Why do you want to add yourself more trouble in life? You are already blind, how are you going to handle the burden of a marriage?" Of course, it was too late for that kind of language to affect my plans, but as I reflected on this reaction later, I wondered what would have been the situation if this had been the first person I had told about my wish to get married.

I did not know much about this man's own married life but, from this reaction, marriage seemed a burden to him and would certainly be an unbearable one to a person who is blind. The years of my married life have proved that is not the case. Marriage provided me not only with a companion but also a pair of eyes, thus largely compensating for my lack of sight. Our four children have been a great source of joy and satisfaction.

Many people with disabilities have met with opposition to marriage from their immediate families, let alone friends like the one in my case. More often, opposition comes from the family of a non-disabled partner motivated by a misguided notion of the immense burden that marriage to a person with disability would impose. Equally unpleasant are situations in my part of the world in which people are forced by over-enthusiastic or anxious parents into union with partners who are not of their own choosing. Although this may have been the case in the past for everyone, whether with or without disability, it is certainly unwarranted when done today on the basis of one's disability.

The church is a major influencing factor in our society. It still commands such great respect, especially in this part of the world, that its influence permeates to both individuals and communities. Its appropriate understanding and interpretation of disability is crucial to how individual church members will relate to persons with disabilities, both spiritually and socially.

Trends in Disability Politics

Samuel Kabue

According to World Health Organization (WHO) global statistics, there are about 600,000,000 persons with disabilities on the earth. These are estimates because many countries, especially those in the developing world, do not keep statistics regarding their populations with disabilities. WHO arrives at these estimates on the premise that at least ten percent of any population is made up of persons with disabilities: sensory, physical, mental or even a combination of two or more of these. Actual statistics are only kept in countries where organized social support exists for planning purposes. The WCC interim theological statement, "A Church of All and for All" notes that what most disabled people around the world do share in common is the experience of being discriminated against. We have been marginalized by patronizing and paternalistic attitudes, made the objects of ridicule and fear, or just ignored and left out. Frequently this treatment has led to a poverty of relationships and opportunities for disabled people and has resulted in economic disenfranchisement. We recognize that there are gross disparities of wealth in different parts of the world, and that a disabled individual in the economic North might live more comfortably than a non-disabled person in the economic South. However, it can still be said that the great majority of disabled people worldwide are in such poor financial circumstances that they are forced to do without many of life's basic necessities.

It is necessary to note that though we are still far from achieving the emancipation of persons with disabilities, their voices are now louder than ever before; they have been joined by allies, friends and relatives to make themselves more visible to governments, service providers and opinion leaders. Whereas the struggle for recognition, acceptance and full involvement rages on, different approaches have needed to be used. The formation and networking of organizations of persons with disabilities all over the world has made it possible to take a civil-rights approach to achieving change. One reason it has taken too long for this to happen is the fact that, although people with disabilities are a most significant minority in the world, they do not enjoy the benefits of living together like minority ethnic or racial groups. They are scattered all over as isolated individual cases. Modern technology, though still not very accessible to the majority, has made it possible to share information and experiences leading to formation of organizations that have grown to be the most important force in addressing issues of disability. It may help briefly to follow the story of how we have arrived at our current position.

I have alluded to the development of approaches to disability, from compassionate care through monasteries' and convents' infirmaries in the Middle Ages to the charitable stage of institutionalized and professional carers. By about the middle of the 19th century, such institutions were quite common in Western Europe and were already gathering momentum in North America. The widening circle of such institutions sponsored by both charities and government departments called for expansion of services from mere care to rehabilitation and education. By the close of the 19th century, a need to have some form of coordination and sharing of experiences at the international level was manifesting itself. In 1920, Rehabilitation International came into being as a forum through which various charities and government bodies could exchange information. This organization has its world congress meetings every four years, organized in different parts of the world as their executive committee decides. It has recently introduced regional congresses since its members continue to increase. We have for instance the Africa chapter of Rehabilitation International where African institutions and government departments in charge of disabilities meet to address disability concerns within their own context.

While these developments were taking place, there was a growing self-awakening of persons with disabilities as they experienced life in institutions. Introduction of formal education opened up a wealth of understanding which led to their beginning to question the type of services they were receiving and to criticize the way they were being treated.

This development gave rise to the formation of their own groups in which they shared their experiences, and this has led to the modern disability movement. The visually impaired seem to have taken the lead in this. The earliest of well-organized groups can be traced in the Nordic countries to such bodies as the Swedish Federation of the Visually Impaired, dating as far back as the beginning of the 20th century. Elsewhere, the strongest of these movements among the blind in particular is the National Federation of the Blind in the United States, which came into being in the 1940s.

By the 1960s, the influence of these organizations had spread elsewhere including some parts of the southern hemisphere, assisting the formation of national associations, which came together to form the International Federation of the Blind (IFB). The formation of the IFB may have been a response to another organization, the World Council for the Welfare of the Blind (WCWB). This was a federation of service-providing organizations whose origin could be traced to the United Kingdom but that had membership all over the world. It needs here be noted that members of the WCWB were mainly charities that had, over time, specialized in fundraising to provide services to persons with disabilities. The boards, management and staff of these charities were not blind themselves, and they organized their programmes according to the way they thought it best for the blind without having to consult them. These types of organizations still exist today, though they are now more accommodating to the participation of the blind. They are referred to as organizations "for" the blind as opposed to those started and managed by the blind people themselves which we refer to as organizations "of" the blind.

In the late 1970s and early 1980s, the movement of the visually impaired as represented by the IFB had noted the wide rift that had developed between their members and those of the service providers under the umbrella of the WCWB. Discussions began to focus into a closer working relationship, and organizations of persons with disabilities considered this move necessary in giving them greater influence on service providers. An amalgamation of the IFB and the WCWB was finally achieved in 1984. One of the difficulties throughout these discussions was what the new organization would be called. There was an open reluctance on the part of both sides to have either the word "for" or "of" in the new name. The name World Blind Union (WBU) was chosen. With time, the WBU has become predominantly an organization "of" the blind due to the way its constitution was framed, requiring its leadership to be made up primarily of blind people. Although it is today the most representative body for the blind or visually impaired at the international level, participation of the former WCWB members or the charities which are largely run by people who are not blind is very limited. Many of them have shied away. The WBU has regional chapters in Europe, Africa and Asia.

Following a similar trend as that of the blind, the deaf too began to organize themselves into self-advocacy groups that developed into national organizations in the first half of the 20th century. They too found the need to join together into a stronger body that would be able to champion their interests through the formation of a widely consultative body. The World Federation of the Deaf came into being in 1951 in Rome, Italy. It now has regional affiliates in various parts of the world

In 1981, a disability movement of considerable potential, Disabled People International (DPI), was born following a major disability conference which took place in Winnipeg, Canada. The DPI is constitutionally a cross-disability movement, and it operated as such in all practical senses for some time. It was seen by many at its formation as a counterbalance to the activities of Rehabilitation International. It did a lot of work in its early years to help the formation of national cross-disability organizations. Unfortunately, the initial leaders of the DPI, despite their good intentions for the inclusion of all, were predominantly the wheelchair-bound. This factor led to questions about representation of the interests of people with other disability such as the blind and the deaf. The emergence of the World Blind Union in 1984 did not make things any better. Later WBU leadership stated strongly that the DPI could not represent the interests of the blind and indirectly discouraged its membership from taking an active part in the DPI. This trend of fragmenting the movement continued when leaders of the World Federation of the Deaf took the same position.

In 1991, a federation was founded which brings together another disability category that is not conventional but whose members have found it helpful to join the movement in order to protest against the stigma attached to them and the discrimination they experience. This was the World Federation of Psychiatric Users. After some years of active work, the federation lost momentum for a while but picked up again after some rigorous restructuring in 1999 when it also changed its name to the World Network of Psychiatric Users and Survivors of Psychiatry.

Another organization that deserves mention is Inclusion International. This is an organization whose mandate is social inclusion of persons with intellectual disabilities. It was founded more than forty years ago under the name of the International League of the Societies of the Mentally Handicapped. Its change of name came as a reflection of the changing trend to reflect a new understanding of this disability and what society needs to do about it. It has to do with the fact that people with intellectual disabilities historically have been the most marginalized. This organization developed through patients' friends and professionals getting together, first as support groups and later as national societies. The organization continues to be led by parents, friends and professionals in the field. This is founded on the understanding that people with intellectual disability, unlike those with sensory or physical disabilities, may not be able to express themselves adequately at certain levels. However, the organization encourages them to participate as far as possible.

The trend in disability politics has brought about a fragmented approach that has not encouraged close working relations across disabilities. This has resulted in a measure of competition for supremacy and recognition. Most of the organizations I have mentioned now have an observer status at the United Nations. In order to speak with one voice, a new organization was established in 1999 at a meeting held in Capetown, South Africa. This was the International Disability Alliance (IDA). The IDA is an alliance of the major world-wide organizations run by and for people with disabilities. Members include Disabled Peoples' International, Inclusion International, the World Blind Union, the World Federation of the Deaf, the World Federation of the Deaf-blind and the World Network of Users and Survivors of Psychiatry.

Originally the IDA was set up as a forum where the presidents of the organizations could share information and strategize on disability advocacy. At the 1999 meeting the decision was made to formalize the IDA as a platform for cooperation between the organizations, as not all of them have presidents. The IDA finds its role in strengthening the voice of people with disabilities at the international level and networking and collaborating on issues of common concern. It should here be mentioned that the IDA remains a very loose alliance which seems to meet only when there is a particular issue of common interest to be addressed.

The UN response

The early participants in the disability arena played a key role in influencing the United Nations to take an interest in disability as a human-rights concern. The entry of the UN has meant greater interaction and an ongoing debate that has in turn attracted many other players, as already seen above. Although the human-rights charter promulgated in 1948 and its subsequent versions clearly indicate that the charter's provisions are meant for all human beings, the unique circumstances of persons with disabilities have led, in the last thirty years or so, to a special focus on them. As part of this ongoing discussion, a number of important documents or UN instruments have been developed through efforts and pressure by these organizations. The first in the series was the 1971 United Nations Declaration of the Rights of Mentally

Retarded Persons. This document called for the recognition of people with mental disability as human beings and called upon the world community to grant them all the entitlements of other human beings. It specifies concerns that are unique to this group and gives guidelines for addressing them. The making of this declaration was influenced by various leaders in the predecessor organization to Inclusion International. This declaration set the pace for more activities at the UN in respect to other disabilities.

Four years later, the 1975 UN Declaration on the Rights of Disabled Persons came into being. This was an expansion of the 1971 declaration to cover not only other disabilities but also to widen the issues covered. Its provisions required that persons with disabilities not only be accorded respect but also be given opportunity for rehabilitation, education, employment, human dignity and enjoyment of life within a family setting.

The momentum picked up as a result of this declaration and led to the UN declaration of 1981 as the International Year for Disabled Persons (IYDP). The theme of the year was full participation and equality. The year was very well publicized all over the world with the notable achievement of creating a lot of awareness. However, it went so fast that by the time it ended there was not much in practical terms that could be seen. This led to a full UN Decade for Persons with Disabilities, 1983-92. In order to ensure that the decade would have the desired impact, a comprehensive document entitled World Programme of Action Concerning Disabled Persons was developed and adopted through a UN resolution in 1982. The document provided guidelines on effective measures for the realization of the goal of full participation of persons with disabilities in social life, development and equality. It was to be implemented at both the international and national levels. At the international level, UN agencies were encouraged to implement the document in accordance with their areas of specialization.

The International Labour Organization (ILO) was one agency that took a practical step, both as a continuation of what it had been trying to do in the area of vocational training and also as a response to the events of the day. It came up with the very first enforceable document for its members who were willing to sign it. This was the Vocational Rehabilitation and Employment (Disabled Persons) Convention, 1983. The essence of the convention was to ensure that appropriate vocational rehabilitation measures were made available to all categories of disabled persons and employment for disabled persons was promoted in the open labour market.

A mid-term observation of the decade and the impact of the World Programme of Action by a panel of experts revealed that the programme was not getting the intended response. Something more binding or convincing was necessary. This observation gave rise to a debate concerning a possible UN convention on persons with disabilities, but the idea was not supported by many of the members of the UN. Instead, it was decided to draw up another document that would develop further the concepts in the World Programme of Action. Persons with disabilities were involved in the writing of this new document which came to be known as the UN Standard Rules on the Equalization of Opportunities for Persons with Disabilities.

This document, which has twenty-two rules on the behaviour of states, was the most comprehensive of all the documents produced up to that time. These rules were divided into four categories. The first included four rules addressing preconditions for equalization of opportunities: awareness-raising, medical care, rehabilitation and support services. The second and probably the most important section covered rules 5 to 12 on target areas of equalization of opportunities. These were identified as accessibility, education, employment, income maintenance and social security, family life and personal integrity, culture, recreation and sports, and religion. The last ten rules defined measures of implementation and mechanisms for monitoring progress. The document was presented to the UN assembly and adopted in December 1993.

Although the rules were simply guidelines that were not binding on governments, the level of awareness built into them caused them to have greater global influence than the World Programme of Action. The early years after their adoption saw many new organizations of persons with disabilities established in many parts of the world. More disability legislation and policies were put in place in different countries than ever before.

Nevertheless, seven years down the road from the adoption of the rules and despite their impact, careful observation showed that a lot of pressure or exceptional good will was necessary to create a real impact and this was possible only in countries where the social environment allowed it. Despite efforts made to increase cooperation, integration and sensitivity to disability issues by governments and other relevant organizations, these attempts at raising awareness were not sufficient to promote full and effective participation and to bring about equalization of opportunities for persons with disabilities in economic, social, cultural and political life. It was felt that there was still need for a more comprehensive and binding instrument to promote and protect the rights and dignity of persons with disabilities. The idea of a convention was once again floated, and through prodigious lobbying work this was accepted in 2003 and an ad hoc committee was put in place made up of governments and non-governmental organizations including organizations of persons with disabilities. This committee is now at work collecting views in the regions as it begins to draft the content of the convention.

Ecumenical response

The ecumenical movement too has, also in the last thirty years or so, found itself faced with the necessity of addressing disability as a concern. After the fourth assembly of the World Council of Churches in 1968, the theme "The Unity of the Church and the Renewal of Humankind" emerged as a means of relating issues of church and society. At the assembly and subsequently, attempts to explore the church as a more inclusive community intensified. A concern to address the inclusion of people with disabilities in the church emerged within the Faith and Order Commission and gathered momentum at the Louvain meeting of the Commission in 1971. This first attempt to address the situation of persons with disabilities came in the form of a theological examination of service for the disabled in light of the compassion of Christ.

The WCC has thus, since the Faith and Order Commission in Louvain, incorporated persons with disabilities in its wider mission and agenda. Efforts have been made to include persons with disabilities and to advocate for their recognition in the member churches. At the WCC's fifth assembly in Nairobi in 1975, the Council reiterated its commitment to the concerns of persons with disabilities through a statement which sought to mobilize the member churches to make similar commitments. The emphasis during this time was on the services and programmes that the Council and member churches could put in place in favour of people with disabilities.

In 1977, a WCC staff task force on persons with disabilities was established to help take further the ideas that had been agreed on in the previous assembly. Two consultations were organized for this purpose which considered various aspects of disability, in Bad Saarow, Germany, and in Sao Paolo, Brazil. From 1978 onwards, the Christian Medical Commission held a series of seven regional conferences on the theme "Health, Healing and Wholeness".

A full-time consultant, Frances Martin, was appointed in 1980 to help the task force raise consciousness among the churches during the United Nations International Year of Disabled Persons. At the WCC's sixth assembly, in Vancouver, Canada, in 1983, there were 21 persons with disabilities, the largest participation in any assembly to that date. Deliberations in the assembly reiterated the need for the churches to accommodate disability concerns in their life and ministry.

In affirming this action, the Council established a disability desk with a full-time member of staff in Geneva in 1984.

A great deal of work in sensitizing churches was carried out for the next seven years. Contacts were re-established with member churches, national and regional ecumenical bodies, church and secular agencies working with persons with disabilities. Unfortunately, the staff position was discontinued in 1991 because of lack of funds. The work was carried out by a task force until 1994 when another staff member was hired on a consultancy basis. Taking over from the task force and with their assistance, this person was responsible for the work until 1996 when the position was again discontinued. Thus, the task force took up the work as the Council prepared for its eighth assembly. One of the most remarkable achievements of the task force at that time was the 1997 central committee statement to the churches. That theological and sociological statement was the first document that was sent out to all the WCC member churches to urge them to consider the question of active involvement by persons with disabilities as part of the churches. The task force worked on the basis of that statement to ensure participation of persons with disabilities in the eighth WCC assembly in Harare, Zimbabwe, in 1998.

The WCC was seeking new ways of carrying out this work at minimum expense and maximum efficiency without necessarily having to establish an expensive structure in Geneva. The vision was to decentralize the work by passing responsibility for certain aspects to other partners with the capacity and willingness to carry out this mandate. During the eighth assembly, ten persons with disabilities from different parts of the world were invited to participate as advisers. In this role, they took the opportunity to hold their own consultations on how best to influence the churches to recognize and incorporate people with disabilities in their witness and service programmes.

The ten advisers decided to form a network known as Ecumenical Disability Advocates Network (EDAN) that would carry the WCC work on disability further in the respective regions from which each individual came. EDAN, as a network and initiative of persons with disabilities, was considered by the WCC a model programme for working with persons with disabilities. The WCC proposed to support this work by identifying an ecumenical partner with both the interest and the working structure necessary for this kind of programme. The National Council of Churches in Kenya was identified as a suitable host, as it was one of the national councils that was already doing some work in partnership with persons with disabilities.

EDAN is therefore a WCC programme and is situated within the Justice, Peace and Creation (JPC) team. Its placement in this team is significant as an acknowledgment that the WCC recognizes disability concerns as justice issues. The network carries out its work in various regions using the WCC's regional structures. Its mandate is to advocate for inclusion, participation and observation of rights of persons with disabilities through networks allied to these structures.

The WCC interim theological statement referred to previously has been the product of nearly three years of consultations and discussions under EDAN with the assistance and guidance of Faith and Order. This *new* interim statement, "A Church of All and for All", is thus a stage on a continuing journey. In developing it, we have benefited from very helpful contributions by a group of disabled individuals – many of whom are ordained ministers or students of theology – and by parents of disabled children and others who experience life alongside people with disabilities in various ways. It is an invitation to the churches to journey with us towards that radical place where all are welcomed at God's banquet table.

The statement is not a comprehensive document but offers pointers and insights on major theological themes. It has very distinct sections on commonalities and differences, hermeneutical issues, *imago Dei*, healing and forgiveness, giftedness and a church for all. These sections have raised the fundamental theological principles on which disability issues need to be viewed in the entire process of being church.

The section on commonalities and differences underscores the need to consider the fact that people with disabilities are individuals with specific characteristics and not a homogeneous group that should be seen merely in terms of provision of assistance and care. The hermeneutical issues section underscores the fact that disabilities need not be viewed either as loss or as punishment for sin. They should be viewed as part of human diversity and the plurality of God's creation.

One over-riding theme in the statement is that of the creation story as reflected by the section on *imago Dei*. This section underscores the fact that it is neither our intellect nor our physical being which reflects the image of God in us. If this were the case, it would contradict the Bible when it says "we are all created in the image of God". We are in a fragile world in which we are all part of the whole that reflects God's image. When God created the entire world, God saw that it was good. Thus, the notion that God's image has to do with our intellect or physical being is a negation of God's purpose. Christ himself bore a broken body on the cross which resulted in our salvation. In whatever state of being, we are wonderfully made – made in the image of God.

The healing section of the statement differentiates between healing and cure. Gospel healing stories are seen not merely as instances of restoration of the body but more as moments when the individual is restored as an integral member of community. When we create an inviting environment and provide space for full participation and active involvement of people with disabilities in the life of church and society, we are participating in Christ's healing ministry.

The giftedness section highlights the fact that all of us, those with and without disabilities, are part of one church and each has gifts and talents to contribute to being church. Each of us has gifts and talents without which the church of Christ is not complete. The section on "a church for all" highlights the necessity of accommodating the needs of all in the worship, social, pastoral and political life of the church. In worship, the statement points out that it will be necessary to consider the needs of different categories of disabilities. This will require good lighting, acoustics, sitting arrangements, sign-language interpretation and access not only to the building but also to the sanctuary. This is what a church for all should involve. It is a church that accommodates everyone, accepts the gifts and talents that everyone brings and welcomes all, irrespective of the differences that may threaten to set us apart from each other.

It is hoped that the text will demystify some of the discourse on disability and will motivate more imaginative thinking about creating communities that encourage and facilitate the full participation of all people, including individuals with disabilities, in the spiritual and social life of the churches.

This document, "A Church of All and for All", was received and adopted by the WCC central committee in August 2003. It has been commended to all the WCC's member churches for study, feedback and planning.

It is not possible to predict with certainty the various reactions to these fundamental theological themes, concerning which there will surely be different interpretations. The purpose of the statement is not to impose any single interpretation but rather to encourage a discourse that will lead to better understanding of persons with disabilities, their needs and aspirations, and to facilitate their full participation and active involvement in the life of the church.

Conclusion

As I have argued previously, religious faiths have been responsible for proclaiming a merciful God who demands that human beings exercise this same virtue. In line with this idea, Christian churches in the past have, especially in the developing countries, established care centres which developed into educational and rehabilitation institutions. These were left in the hands of carers who too often maintained them in isolation from whatever else happened in the society. Those in such institutions remained closed off and therefore were strangers to the rest of society. This background has partly been responsible for a situation in which society at large is ill-prepared for social integration.

As the WCC's interim statement on disability notes, it is a fact that despite many years of addressing this issue, the church has been a constituent part of a world where we have set up walls. Walls that shut people in or shut people out. Walls that prevent people from meeting and talking to others. Walls that keep too many people from participating fully in life. Many people with disabilities still find themselves isolated behind walls of shame and fear, walls of ignorance and prejudice, walls of anger, walls of rigid dogma and cultural misunderstanding. This sad situation contradicts the reality that the church is called to be one body. The churches must become more conscious of the walls around us, if we are to answer the call to become one body through full participation.

A Church of All and for All
An Interim Statement

This statement was prepared for the central committee of the World Council of Churches, meeting 26 August-2 September 2003 in Geneva, by the Ecumenical Disability Advocates Network (EDAN) and has been commended to the churches for study, feedback and action.

Introduction

As the author of the letter to the Ephesians stressed: Christ came to tear down the walls (Eph. 2:14). Whenever we consider the ways in which to respond to issues of disability, we do well to remember the walls that we have set up. All of these walls are so human, yet they contradict Christ's ministry of reconciliation; walls that shut people in or shut people out; walls that prevent people from meeting and talking to others. In days gone by, people with disabilities were actually kept behind walls, inside institutions. Now we are all a part of mainstream society. It is estimated that some 600 million people are persons with disabilities. Yet people, especially persons with disabilities, still find themselves isolated. Now there are walls of shame; walls of prejudice; walls of hatred; walls of competition; walls of fear; walls of ignorance; walls of theological prejudice and cultural misunderstanding. The church is called to be an inclusive community, to tear down the walls. This interim statement is an invitation to journey towards making that more of a reality. It has been written by disabled people, parents and others who experience life alongside them in various ways.

Historically, disability has been interpreted as loss, as something that illustrates the human tragedy. The stories in the gospels about how Jesus healed persons with different diseases and disabilities are traditionally interpreted as acts of liberation, stories of how human beings receive possibilities to live a richer life. From that time, churches have often wrestled with how best to exercise an appropriate ministry for, to and with persons with disabilities.

The ecumenical movement also found itself faced with the necessity of addressing the issue. After the fourth assembly of the World Council of Churches in 1968, the theme "The Unity of the Church and the Renewal of Humankind" emerged as a means of relating issues of church and society. At the assembly and subsequently, the attempt to explore the church as a more inclusive community intensified. A concern to address the inclusion of handicapped people in the church emerged within the Faith and Order Commission, and gathered momentum at the Louvain meeting of the Commission in 1971. This first attempt to address the situation of persons with disabilities was a theological examination of service for the disabled in the light of the compassion of Christ.

In the period which followed, concern with persons with disabilities moved from theological reflection to practical questions of inclusiveness within churches and church communities. But often, this reflection and action in the churches treated "persons with handicaps" and "the differently abled" and "persons with a disability" (all those terms were designed to reflect inclusiveness and each replaced the other) as objects rather than subjects of reflection. The appearance of EDAN (Ecumenical Disability Advocates Network), founded at the WCC's 1998 assembly, and its assimilation within the WCC structures in the Justice, Peace and Creation team, has itself come to be a sign of hope in the process of conscientization of Christian churches and institutions, because now persons with disabilities are themselves the subjects or actors of reflection or action. EDAN works in the eight regions of the world and serves as a network of encounter and support as persons with disabilities seek to address the specific issues and challenges in their own contexts.

However, there has been a growing awareness in some churches that persons with disabilities invite the church to explore anew the understanding of the gospel and the nature of the church. This awareness was evident in a first interim statement at the 1997 central committee of the WCC which sought to reflect theologically and engage the churches in acting to be more inclusive communities. This new interim statement, drawn up with participation from the Faith and Order Commission, is thus a stage on a continuing journey. It is not comprehensive but offers pointers and insights on major theological themes. It is hoped that the statement will also enable the churches to interact with the disability discourse and help them address inclusion, active participation and full involvement in the spiritual and social life of the church in particular and society in general.

Persons with disabilities – commonalities and differences

1. "The disabled" have struggled hard to become recognized as "disabled people". The fight was worthwhile for two reasons. First, throughout history, disabled people have been depersonalized and perceived as a problem to be dealt with. Second, they are often seen as a homogeneous group whose individual differences do not need to be respected. This section is about who we are, our common experience. Its purpose is to make the point that, in common with

all groups in society, we too are very diverse and have different stories. We also want to explore a possible framework to help disabled people and the churches to find a common starting point from which to begin this exploration.

2. We have probably all experienced limitations; in how we move, feel, think, perceive. Due to our impairments and resultant disabilities, we have been marginalized by the attitudes, actions or barriers in society. In many societies, persons with disabilities have organized themselves into powerful lobby groups which advocate against such marginalization and for disability rights and independence, even from their familial carers. Yet one of the hardest challenges facing many carers[1] is to maintain the voice of the voiceless when those for whom they care often have such profound and multiple disabilities that their silence is only understood in the depth of the loving relationship of care.

3. Modern society has brought with it many hazards that clearly make humankind collectively responsible for injuries caused by the likes of landmines and substance abuse, but the cause of some disabilities remains inexplicable.

4. Most disabled people are economically disenfranchised and experience some deprivation in their standard of living or employment opportunities. Carers also have to make considerable sacrifices, experiencing significant demands on their time and resources that limit their ability to pursue other activities and careers. Yet, to protest against the economic deprivation of disabled people and their carers in a global context is to grossly under-estimate the relativity of poverty between societies and countries. The disparity between the material situation of a disabled person in the economic North and that of a non-disabled person in the economic South (the former may be "better off" than the latter) should not be ignored. Those factors represent the existential bond and reality facing the overwhelming majority of persons with disabilities and their families today.

5. Disability can cause not only economic disenfranchisement but also poverty of relationships and opportunity. Persons with disabilities often become vulnerable to discriminatory social trends. A

---

[1] In the UK, the term "carers" denotes people who offer care because of an emotional bond usually for little or no financial recompense. There are, in fact, national associations of carers which offer mutual support and encouragement. Professional care-givers are distinguished by a variety of nomenclatures. This may contrast with other cultures which may use terms like familial care-givers, etc.

market economy encourages abortion and the allowing of babies to die. In many countries the systematic abortion of the foetus with certain malformations and those with Down's syndrome gives a very negative message of society's view of disability. Such a market economy further leads to institutionalization and reduced access to adequate medical care for the majority of the world's population. Disabled people become vulnerable to easy commercial fixes and religious groups which offer miraculous healing in the setting of superficial acceptance and friendship.

6. No social group is ever the same, and disabled people are no exception to the rule. We come from a variety of cultures, and are thus culturally conditioned in the same manner as every person. We have experienced different kinds and levels of medical care and differing social attitudes. We have come to an acceptance of our disabilities by diverse routes. Some of us have been disabled since birth, either by congenital conditions or by the trauma of birth itself, whilst others have been victims of accidents or have had disabilities develop later in life. Each one of us has struggled to accept our disability and has found that we have been accepted or hindered in this acceptance by the quality of medical care or education we have received, or by the attitudes of people who have had an influence in our lives and spiritual well-being. We have been supported by the bonds of different disability cultures such as the uniqueness of sign-language or a particular political understanding of our minority status. We wish to assert that our differences are part of the richness of disabled people as a group, and that we rejoice in them.

7. Those disabled people who share a Christian faith are united by their awareness of God's love and Jesus' compassion for sick and disabled people, and find strength in the care of Christ. However, many have found that the church's teaching on this truth has been too limited, and have looked for their own understanding. Each one's awareness of how long he/she might expect to live and their own faith experience have affected how they accept their disabilities. They have relied upon certain theological tools to address their existential need to explain the mystery and paradox of love and suffering, coexisting and giving meaning to their lives.

8. We affirm that God loves all disabled people and extends to all the opportunity to respond to that love. We believe that every disabled person has the opportunity to find peace with God.

9. Genesis 32:24-26: We quote: "Jacob was left alone, and a man wrestled with him until daybreak. When the man saw that he did not prevail against Jacob, he struck him on the hip socket, and

Jacob's hip was put out of joint as he wrestled with him. Then he said, 'Let me go, for the day is breaking.' But Jacob said, 'I will not let you go unless you bless me.'"

10. In our wrestling with God, as disabled people we all ask the same basic questions, but the theological enquiry involved may be complex. Why me or my loved one? Is there a purpose to my disability? The answers to those questions can be influenced by the expected time-span of a disability, and by the time and circumstances of its onset. Acceptance or otherwise of a disabling impairment is influenced by knowledge of how long one can expect to live and what quality of life one can expect to experience.

11. We have wrestled with God intellectually and physically to achieve this peace, and whilst some of us have been privileged to write intellectually about it, others have shown it in their innate gift of grace which is shown in the love and affection to those who care for them so deeply. If so many disabled people have this ability to come to terms with God, the church must surely find ways of accepting the gifts which we have to offer. It is not a case of meeting halfway but of full acceptance.

Hermeneutical issues

12. How can we interpret from a theological perspective the fact that some people live with disabilities? What does that fact tell us about human life in God's world? We have learned from 20th-century philosophy and theology that we are historical beings and our interpretations are always made from within history. Our interpretations of reality are always finite because we are finite beings. When we are developing a theological interpretation of the fact of human disabilities, we must acknowledge that history has changed and will change the way we interpret it. And by history, we may mean the story of an individual, or the developing perceptions of the community in which persons with disabilities live.

13. As has been noted above, disability has historically been interpreted as loss, an example of the tragedies that human beings can experience. The gospel stories about how Jesus heals persons with different diseases and disabilities are traditionally interpreted as illustrating how human beings are liberated and empowered to live a richer life.

14. In this understanding, people with disabilities are seen as weak and needing care. As a result, they are viewed as objects for charity, those who receive what other persons give. Thus, people

with disabilities cannot meet other people in the churches on equal terms. They are regarded as somehow less than fully human.

15. The church has justified this view from different theological perspectives. For instance, disability has been interpreted as a punishment for sins, either committed by the persons with disabilities themselves or by their relatives in earlier generations. Or disability has been understood as a sign of lack of faith that prevents God from performing a healing miracle. Or disability has been understood as a sign of demonic activity, in which case exorcism is needed to overcome the disability. Such interpretations have led to the oppression of people with disabilities in the churches. In that respect, the churches' attitudes have reflected attitudes in societies as a whole. Structures of oppression within societies and churches have mutually reinforced each other.

16. When new ways to understand disability have emerged in society, new theological ways to understand this issue have also emerged in the churches and in the ecumenical movement. But the churches have not taken a leading role here. Even though one can find inspiration for such an approach in the Bible, they have not been a prophetic voice against oppression. Rather, churches have generally followed the trends in society, often with distinct reluctance. Conservative structures in the churches, often related to the churches' own charitable institutions, have enforced old ways of interpreting disability. Theological ideas like that linking disability and divine punishment for sins remain evident in every part of the world, and disabled persons have been subjected to "pastoral counselling" to address the presumed causes of their "punishment".

17. When new understandings of disabilities emerge in society, traditional theological interpretations are challenged. In some churches, this has raised awareness that people with disabilities were not seen as equal. In many churches, traditional ways of treating people with disabilities were then perceived as oppressive and discriminatory, and actions towards people with disabilities moved from "charity" to recognition of their human rights. Changing attitudes have led to new questions and interpretations. Awareness has slowly grown that people with disability have experienced that which can enrich the churches themselves. In the search for unity and inclusion, some have acknowledged that people with disability must be included in the life and the witness of the churches. Often, this has been connected to the language about weakness found in the New Testament, especially in the two epistles to the Corinthians.

18. But even this insight has been challenged. Is disability really something that shows the weaknesses in human life? Is that in itself a limiting and oppressive interpretation? Do we not have to take another, more radical step? Is disability really something that is limiting? Is the language of disability as a "loss" an adequate one at all, despite it being a stage of the journey undertaken by persons with disabilities themselves? Is a language of plurality not more adequate? To live with a disability is to live with other abilities and limitations that others do not have. All human beings live with limitations. Is not disability something that God has created in order to build a plural, and richer, world? Is not disability a gift from God rather than a limiting condition with which some persons have to live?

19. Such questions need to be taken seriously when we are searching for a new theological understanding of disability. This interim statement is an ongoing process. We will never reach the point where we find "the" theological understanding. We must acknowledge the fact that we will have a different way of raising the theological perspectives tomorrow than we have today. The main purpose of an interim statement is not to impose one understanding of disability, but to enable us to engage in an ongoing conversation. It is the process in itself that is valuable. It can be liberating both for the churches and people with disabilities.

20. Disability is a human condition and, as such, it is ambiguous. To be human is to live a life that is marked both by the God-given good of creation and the brokenness that is a part of human life. We experience both sides of human life with disabilities. To interpret disability from one of these perspectives is to deny the ambiguity of life and to create an artificial ontological split in the heart of our understanding of disability.

21. We have to let different and conflicting interpretations stand beside each other and let them challenge and correct each other. We should not try to create a synthesis that removes the conflict between the different interpretations. Rather, we should hold on to the tension between them as that which keeps the process going.

Imago Dei

22. In the history of Christian theology, the notion that humanity is made in the image of God has tended to mean that it is the mind or soul which is in God's image, since the bodily (corporeal or physical) aspect of human nature can hardly represent the incorporeal, spiritual reality of the transcendent God. We should not

underestimate the profound reaction against idolatry in early Christianity; no animal or human form should be taken to represent God who is invisible. However, the perceived kinship between our minds and God's mind (or Logos), coupled with the assumed analogy between the incarnation of God's Logos in Christ and the embodiment of the (immortal) soul/mind in the human person, encouraged a predominantly intellectual interpretation of how human beings are made in the image of God.

23. This tendency may at times have permitted the positive acceptance of intelligent persons with physical disabilities: e.g., Didymus the Blind (4th century) was nick-named Didymus the See-er because he saw more profoundly than those with physical sight. It has also encouraged positive (if somewhat patronizing) responses to persons with profound and multiple disabilities on the grounds that "you can see the soul peeping out through their eyes". But this understanding of human nature is both inherently elitist and dualist. It ultimately tends to exclude those whose mental or physical incapacities profoundly affect their entire personality and existence.

24. More recently, the notion that humanity is made in the image of God is taken to mean that each of us is made in the image of God and, therefore, each of us deserves to be equally respected. It conspires with modern human-rights ideologies to encourage individuals to assert their right to a decent deal in society, and to recognition of each person's inherent dignity, no matter what his/her race, religion or impairment.

25. This tendency has had a positive impact in encouraging respect for those who are not white, male, able-bodied and intelligent. But it has also exacerbated the prejudice that we should all be perfect since we are made in God's image. Obvious failure to reach such notional perfection then becomes problematic. How can this person, who apparently has physical or mental defects, be made in God's image? The modernist rights approach may challenge the attitudes of some past traditional societies, but the success-oriented values of modern individualism encourage an interpretation of *imago Dei* which, we would argue, does not take account of core elements in Christian theology.

26. The phrase we are examining occurs in the Genesis narrative of the creation of Adam. So there are two important features that need to be taken seriously. First, Adam represents the whole human race. The very name Adam means man-humanity in the generic sense, for the creation of Eve from his rib represents sexual

differentiation in the human race. Secondly, while Adam was indeed made in the image and likeness of God, this was marred by his disobedience, classically known as the Fall. Some early theologians suggested that he retained the image but lost the likeness. The point here is that glib theological talk about being made in God's image needs to be countered with a sensitivity to the corporate nature of that image, and the fact that all have fallen short of the glory (image) of God (Rom. 3:23).

27. For the Christian community, this reflection on Genesis 1 is confirmed by the New Testament. A reading of Paul's epistles soon shows that the dynamic of salvation depends upon the parallel between Adam and Christ. Adam is the "old man", Christ the "new man" (Rom. 5:2; 2 Cor. 5:17), and all of us (male and female) are in Adam and potentially in Christ (Rom. 7; 1 Cor. 15:22). Both are in some sense corporate figures. In Christ we are a new creation, but as in Adam all die, so in Christ all will be made alive. In a sense, Christ alone is the true image of God; the image of God in Adam (the old humanity) was marred. So we are in God's image because we are in Christ.

28. If Christ is the true image of God, then radical questions have to be asked about the nature of the God who is imaged. At the heart of Christian theology is a critique of success, power and perfection, and an honouring of weakness, brokenness and vulnerability.

29. Being in Christ is being in the body of Christ. This is essentially a corporate image; a body is made up of many members, all of whom bring different contributions to the whole (1 Cor. 12; Rom. 12). Indeed, the weak limbs (members), and even those body parts we are ashamed of and cover up (see the Greek of 1 Cor. 12:23), are indispensable and are to be especially honoured, their essential contribution recognized. Furthermore, this is a physical image, and the physical reality was that in his bodily existence, Christ was abused, disabled and put to death. Some aspects of God's image in Christ can only be reflected in the church as the body of Christ by the full inclusion and honouring of those who have bodies that are likewise impaired.

30. We would therefore argue that: (1) Christian theology needs to interpret the *imago Dei* from a Christological and soteriological (the saving work of Christ for the world) standpoint, which takes us beyond the usual creationist and anthropological perspectives. (2) Christian theology needs to embrace a non-elitist, inclusive understanding of the body of Christ as the paradigm for understanding

the *imago Dei*. (3) Without the full incorporation of persons who can contribute from the experience of disability, the church falls short of the glory of God, and cannot claim to be in the image of God.

Without the insight of those who have experience of disability, some of the most profound and distinctive elements of Christian theology are easily corrupted or lost.

31. "When any one of us, or a group of us, is excluded because of some lack of ability, we are prevented from using our God-given gifts to make Christ's body complete. Together, let us make the beautiful mosaic that God intends" (Norma Mengel on mental illness).

32. The study of the Bible as the source of Christian theological reflection and as the revelation of the purpose of God, and the knowledge of the Creator, leads us to the certainty that we have accepted and been accepted by a God of Love. It is God who encourages us to live in the light of his Son with our errors, afflictions and disabilities. The prophet Isaiah points to the One who carries all our afflictions (Isa. 53:4-6). The God "who shows no partiality" (Gal. 2:6) includes everyone in his bosom, male or female, whatever their physical or mental conditions.

Disabilities and healing

33. However, the scriptures speak not only of the God who identifies himself with human affliction, but also the One who exercised a ministry of healing and wholeness. How does this relate to the continuing witness of persons with disabilities? We cannot deal with the relationship between healing and disability without asking the following questions: What does it mean to talk about the image of God in relation to persons with disability? If the image is described as "perfect body", or "perfect reason", how can persons with disability embrace such an image of God? What is the relationship between our theological language and practice with regard to the issue of disability? How much of the medical and social language which treats persons with disability as objects determines both academic theologies and general attitudes about and towards persons with disability as objects of pity, forgiveness and healing? How far do we have a holistic understanding of healing which integrates the moral, the spiritual and the physical? Furthermore, we want to raise questions about what it means to call the church the body of Christ. Can persons who are visually impaired or who have a body with cerebral palsy be included? Although many Christians

consciously deny any relationship between disability and sin (which also includes suffering), some of their attitudes seem to reflect such a link.

34. "Wherefore, when we now attempt to speak of that image, we speak of a thing unknown; an image which we not only have never experienced all our lives, and experience still. Of this image, therefore, all we now possess are mere terms – the image of God!... But there was, in Adam, an illumined reason, a true knowledge of God and a will the most upright to love both God, and his neighbour" (Luther).

35. From a disability perspective of a hermeneutic of suspicion, it is obvious that persons with some form of disability cannot accept the image of God defined thus. For example, persons with some form of mental disability or some form of learning disability will be disqualified as human beings because they will not reflect the definition of the image of God as soul, as reason or as rationality. A hermeneutic of suspicion cannot accept the image of God or soul as reason or rationality. It is also obvious that these interpretations of the image of God or soul as rationality are inconsistent with other world-views, e.g. African.

36. Traditional definitions of healing, wholeness and holiness (based on a particular theological anthropology of God, the image of God, and the body of Christ which, in turn, is based on cultural images of beauty and perfection with regard to the image of God and the body of Christ) are extremely unhelpful, especially during the celebration of the eucharist. Such theologies sometimes treat healing as metaphor in very exclusive and victimizing ways to persons with disabilities.

37. In the case of disability, it is often assumed that healing is either to eradicate the problem as if it were a contagious virus, or that it promotes virtuous suffering, or a means to induce greater faith in God. Such theological approaches to healing either emphasize "cure" or "acceptance" of a condition.

38. Other definitions of healing make a clear theological distinction between healing and curing. Healing refers to the removal of oppressive systems, whereas curing has to do with the physiological reconstruction of the physical body. For some theologians, Jesus' ministry was one of healing and not curing.

39. In this kind of theology, disability is a social construct, and healing is the removal of social barriers. From these perspectives, the healing stories in the gospels are primarily concerned with restoration of the persons to their communities, not the cure of their

physiological conditions. For example, the man with leprosy in Mark 1:40-45 who asks Jesus to make him clean is mainly asking Jesus to restore him to his community. In like manner, in Mark 2:1-12, Jesus met the paralytic and forgave him his sins.

40. Forgiving sins here means removing the stigma imposed on him by a culture in which disabilities were associated with sin. Hence this man was ostracized as sinful and unworthy of his society's acceptance. In these healing stories Jesus is primarily removing societal barriers in order to create accessible and accepting communities.

41. The good news of the gospel from this perspective is that it creates inclusive communities by challenging oppressive and dehumanizing systems and structures. Africans, for example, might argue that theologians who pursue this line of exploration are engaging in theological reductionism of healing from a scientific viewpoint. A Western scientific world-view might argue that the medical conditions described in the biblical narratives could not be physiologically cured by divine intervention. Some theologians would even argue that the dispensation of such types of healing ended with the advent of Western scientific medicine.

42. It must be noted that Jesus did not make a distinction between social restoration and physical healing. Both always happened at any given time of healing. Consequently, the integral relationship of health, salvation and healing is an imperative for a holistic theological interpretation of disability. That requires a different theological discourse on the body of Christ and the image of God from the perspectives of persons with disability.

43. The biblical healing narratives are important bases for a theological hermeneutic of disability. However, one must try to engage in such an investigation without falling into another theological pitfall: what Nancy Lane calls "victim theology". Victim theologies tend to either blame persons for their lack of faith, which accounts for their disabilities not being healed; accuse persons of possessing demons, which must be exorcised; say that through the sufferings of persons with disability, God shows forth God's glory and power; or blame disability on either the sins of parents or of disabled people themselves.

44. Victim theologies "... place the burden for healing on the person who is disabled, causing further suffering and continued alienation from faith communities" (Lane).

45. For persons with disability, the relationship between healing and disability is both ambivalent and ambiguous. While for other

theologians, there is an obvious definition of healing evident in the Bible, for persons with disability healing is tentative, relative, ambivalent, ambiguous and ongoing. Healing can bring joy and relief. It can also bring pain, frustration, and serious theological questions.

46. A straightjacket understanding of healing in general and the biblical healing narratives in particular makes discussion of healing in relation to disability very difficult. It is obvious that the main danger to avoid is to treat healing, especially healing with respect to disability, to justify our favourable notion of healing without any reference to the totality of the *raison d' être* of Christian theology. To discuss healing either from socio-economic emancipation or physical body reparation perspectives, or from psychological/spiritual perspectives is to engage in distracting and speculative arguments as to the kind of healing Jesus carried out and why.

47. A theological statement of healing with respect to disability needs to be made with reference to the history of salvation. Salvation history is here defined as the self-revelation of God then, now, and in the future through events and acts through which God transforms, empowers, renews, reconciles and liberates God's creation and everything therein made possible by the work of the Holy Spirit. Such a theology is evident in holy scripture.

48. It is against the background of salvation history that a definition of healing from the perspective of disability is attempted. But there is also a need to give a working definition of disability, based on which healing is also defined. In Genesis 1:25b, God pronounced creation as good. It was good, for God has enacted salvation history in creation in which God will continue to transform, renew, reconcile and liberate creation. God's creating and saving acts are concurrent. An illustration with the body will help to make this point clear. When we are well, there is within the body provision of antibodies to prevent illness as well as to produce more antibodies to fight viruses and bacteria that will make us sick.

49. Disability in this theological understanding is a negation of God's intention for his creation to be good. Disability in all its forms and causes is a negation of God's good intention. Similarly, all negative attitudes, systems and structures that exclude and prevent or contribute in any way to the exclusion of persons with disability do not actualize God's intended good of God's creation.

50. Healing then is an act, event, system and structure which encourages, facilitates God's empowering, renewing, reconciling and liberating processes in order to reverse the negation of God's

intended good for God's creation. Therefore, the overall theological contribution of the healing narratives in the New Testament is to demonstrate or serve as signs of God's salvation history. God wills the acceptance and inclusion of each in a community of interdependence where each supports and builds up the other, and where each lives life to the full according to their circumstances and to the glory of God.

Each human being a gift

51. All life is a gift from God, and there is an integrity to this creation. We read in Genesis (1:31) that after creating all of heaven and earth and every form of life, God saw that "... indeed, it was very good". God did not say it was "perfect". With the breath of life, God has imbued each person with dignity and worth. We believe that humanity is "created in the image and likeness of God" (Gen. 1:26), with each human bearing aspects of that divine nature yet no one of us reflecting God fully or completely. Being in God's image does not just mean bearing this likeness, but the possibility of becoming as God intends.

52. This includes all people, whatever their abilities or impairments. It means that every human being is innately gifted and has something to offer that others need. This may be simply one's presence, one's capacity to respond to attention, to exhibit some sign of appreciation and love for other people. Each has something unique to contribute (1 Cor. 12:12-27) and should thus be considered as a gift. We cannot speak about this "giftedness" without also speaking about each person's limitations. They are the basis of our need of each other and of God, irrespective of the labelling of our abilities. Living in this interdependence opens us to one another and to a deeper, more honest, self-knowledge, and so makes us each more fully human, more fully people of communion, more fully realizing the *imago Dei* we bear.

53. Besides the innate gifts of relationship that are inherent in each person, most people with disabilities have other gifts to contribute to the life of the community and church. These are as varied as the many different parts of the human body, but all are necessary to the whole. They include natural abilities in perception and movement; talents and skills developed through education and training in areas such as academic disciplines, religion, science, business, athletics, technology, medicine and the arts. While many gifts are brought to fruition throughout an individual's life-time, some may never be realized due to circumstances, including the presence of

disability. We need one another for our gifts to be revealed. A person who has suffered rejection or has been devalued may not show or share many of her own gifts or his own contribution to humanity, unless he/she is shown full acceptance and unconditional love. In our relationships, it is our task to call out the gifts of each other so that each person's potential may be realized and God may be glorified.

54. Individuals with disabilities, as well as their families, friends and carers/care-givers, may also have gifts to share that have emerged precisely fro m the experience of living with disability. Individuals with disabilities know what it is to have one's life turned upside-down by the unexpected. We have found ourselves in that liminal space between what is known and what is yet unknown, able only to listen and wait. We have faced fear and death and know our own vulnerability. We have met God in that empty darkness, where we realized we were no longer "in control" and learned to rely on God's presence and care. We have learned to accept graciously and to give graciously, to be appreciative of the present moment. We have learned to negotiate a new terrain, a new way of life that is unfamiliar. We have learned to be adaptable and innovative, to use our imaginations to solve new problems. We can be resilient. We know what it is to live with ambiguity and in the midst of paradox, that simplistic answers and certitudes do not sustain us. We have become skilful in areas we never expected to master. We have become accidental experts with skills and expertise to share with the wider community and church.

55. While people with disabilities are endowed with gifts, we are also called to be a gift, to give ourselves to God's service. God wants our whole being, for us to give all of ourselves, to hold nothing back. That includes the disability (the impairment). It is not something of which to be ashamed or to be kept hidden at all cost. For a disabled person, the impairment is one attribute of who he/she is, and is to be included as part of the "holy and acceptable" offering of the self. However, just as it would be wrong to deny the reality of disability as part of our lives, it is also wrong to attribute more honour and recognition to a person's contributions just because he or she also happens to have a disability.

Challenges to theology

56. The part of this statement that dealt with a theological understanding said no to any reductionist tendencies in our way of interpreting stories about healing miracles in the gospels. It chal-

lenged us to make our theological understanding so broad, so spacious, that it could take into account every aspect of human life in relation to Christ's saving grace. Jesus came that we should have life and have it abundantly (John 1:10) and in him all things will be united (Eph. 1:10). This vision of unity in Jesus Christ challenges us to say no to every form of reductionism and to view life in its full richness and complexity. All theology is *theologia viatorum*, a theology of the road, and that is why this statement can only be an interim statement. In relation to disability, theology is challenged to talk about God, faith and life in a way open to God's future; that can surprise us all, and unite and transcend every human existence. A theological understanding of disability has to interpret this issue in the context of the *unfinished* history of God's salvation.

57. People with disabilities, and particularly people with learning disabilities, disturb and confuse the accepted order in many societies. Disabled people disturb human notions of perfection, purpose, reward, success and status; they also disturb notions of a God who rewards virtue with health and prosperity. The responses to this disturbance can be pity as expressed by charitable works, or banishment (putting people away out of sight and mind), and/or fear. Whatever the basis of the response, disabled people are given no meaningful place in society.

58. The presence of disability in our lives directly challenges fundamental assumptions and stereotypes acquired over time. We often cloak the reality of disability in a shroud of silence, or respond with demeaning pity, ridicule or hate. The way we respond to persons with disabilities is essential to the message of the cross.

59. As Christians, we worship a God who became flesh and hung motionless and utterly incapacitated on the cross. Ours is a God of vulnerability and woundedness. Yet often, we choose to forego or forget the crucifixion, preferring to turn directly to the resurrection. Christ rose from the dead with his wounds. We too discover him in our wounds, and we discern his presence in our vulnerability and in our courage to live the lives we have been given.

60. For us Christians, the cross of Jesus Christ is a symbol of life. When the Word became flesh (John 1:14), it was the broken flesh of humanity that was assumed. Even when Christ rose from the dead, he did so with the wounds that he suffered on the cross (Luke 24:36-39). And when St Paul confessed his own thorn in the flesh, he received the revelation that God's strength is perfected in weakness (2 Cor. 12:7-8). Indeed, long before any of the gospel miracles of healing, perhaps the earliest account of God's word

being heard through disability is the example of Moses' speech impairment in Exodus (4:10-17). Here is an example of a person with a particular disability being chosen by God – not simply in spite of his disability, but with his disability – to be a leader among the people of Israel.

61. Finally, at the last supper and in our liturgies that recall that event, we repeat the words of Christ holding before us, for the life of the world, his own damaged and disabled body: "Take, eat; this is my body, which is broken for you" (cf. Matt. 26:26).

62. As Paul asserted, "We have this treasure in clay pots" (2 Cor. 4:7). The treasure is secreted in human bodies. God took dust, turned it into clay. The breath or spirit of God was contained in the clay vessel. Treasure is secreted in ordinariness, the image of God in ordinary human being. Paul's reference in the previous verse to God's creative word, "let light shine out of darkness", reinforces the cross-reference to the creation narrative. The treasure is the divine light which has shone in our hearts to give us the knowledge of the glory of God in the face of Jesus Christ.

63. Our ministry to children and adults with disability presents us with more than a chance to serve our neighbour. It presents us with a challenge to our culture where a worldly image (rather than God's image) is a priority, where ideal perfection is valued and weakness criticized, and where virtues alone are emphasized and failures are concealed. Ours is a witness to the centrality and visibility of the cross in our lives.

64. Another fundamental challenge to theology is a misguided understanding of forgiveness. Misconceptions of old, often affirmed in the Judaeo-Christian scriptures and confirmed throughout Christian history, have led us at times to connect disability with shame, sin or a lack of faith. This is a difficult myth to dispel. When we are tempted to consider disability as punishment or a test from God, we need to think differently. When families are weighed down by such feelings imposed on them by cultural attitudes, we must be swift to awaken them and ourselves to the reality taught by Christ. When asked about the man born with blindness, Christ responded: Neither those with disabilities nor their families have sinned. But the persons who have a disability are born into this world in order that God's works might be revealed in them (John 9:3, paraphrase).

65. Each of us is born the way that we are, with the gifts that we each have, as well as with our inadequacies, in order that God's works might be revealed in us. When we think of forgiveness, we

most often think of guilt and redemption. Yet the contemporary Greek word for forgiveness is *synchoresis*. The word literally means "fitting together" *(syn-chore-sis)*, "sharing the same space" or "making space for all people". Perhaps such an understanding will help us to disassociate disability from sin and guilt.

Struggling with disabled people for their full realization

66. At the beginning of the 21st century, as was the case before the Christian era, sectors of the population who are unable to compete or to perform at the levels that society demands are vitiated, despised or, in more contemporary terms, discarded. Among them, we find a high proportion of people with sensorial, motor and mental disabilities.

67. We will find them living in any of the great cities of the world: men and women of all ages, ethnic backgrounds, colours, cultures and religions who, because they have a disability, live in abject poverty, hunger, dependence, preventable disease and maltreatment by those who are "able".

68. It is the role of the church in this new century to face the reality of humanity in the image of a disabled Jesus; the reality of people with disabilities who are rejected and abandoned.

69. It is painful that the churches throughout the world have not addressed more vigorously the sufferings of marginalized, poor, blind, deaf, and physically and mentally limited people. We do not need pity, or mercy, but compassionate understanding and opportunities to develop our vocations, possibilities and abilities.

70. In their efforts to attain peace, preserve the environment, ensure the equality of women and the rights of the child, care for the aged, churches and Christians should also include the struggle for the full realization of disabled persons in their agendas. "Truly I tell you: anything you did for one of my brothers here, however insignificant, you did for me" (Matt. 25:40).

71. Over the past twenty years, positive attitudes towards disability and disabled persons have increased in our churches and Christian institutions. While far from being universal, this is a welcome development.

72. But it is important to be aware that, in some parts of the world and in some churches, there has recently been a return towards over-protection and even disregard of disabled persons. In some places, we have been manipulated by evangelical groups. Even worse than being ignored, manipulating disabled people could become the church's new sin.

Church for all: community

73. Perhaps when Jesus compared the reign of God to a king who prepares a banquet for his elite friends, He was remembering the passage in Isaiah (Isa. 25:6-7). Certainly many people who live with disability in themselves or loved ones have at times felt that a pall has been thrown over their lives, that they are considered a disgrace to their communities! In Matthew's account of this story, the king's intended guests are too caught up in their personal affairs to heed his summons. But he does not postpone the banquet. Instead, he invites whoever else happens to be around at the moment. Jesus did not say God's reign was for a future world; he said, "The kingdom of God is at hand." It is a present reality; respond to it now! It is no longer the elite who are being summoned; rather, the presence of all those who have been ignored, forgotten and left out is requested. When all are invited to this feast, to this church, the list will include people with physical and mental impairments and chronic illness. How does it affect our worship if, instead of inviting only those whose patterns of behaviour, speech and preferences are known, we extend an open invitation to all? What is the message for our congregations today?

74. The most evident expression of the gathering of the community is the common worship of the congregation. For the liturgy to be truly the work of the people and to accommodate the participation of all the gathered body in worship, we may need to be reminded of what God said long ago: "Enlarge the site of your tent, and let the curtains of your habitations be stretched out" so there is room for everyone (Isa. 54:2). We may need to reconfigure our space, reimagine how we do liturgy, reconsider the role each person plays. Both the drama of liturgy and the drama of disability deal with the fragility of our lives and our dependence upon God. We need to be able to bring our struggles into our worship so that the symbols of the liturgy will be meaningful to us. Symbolically, this is God's banquet table. Have we made it possible for everyone who so desires to get there, to partake of the feast, and to join the conversation? In this gathered body, will there be a place for each person? To ensure that all can participate in worship means we need to consider how our experience and expression of liturgy engages the whole person; physical movement, senses and intellect. People with learning difficulties respond to the integrity of a congregation. They pick up the real and true involvement of those around them, and respond to that devotion.

75. Great significance has been ascribed to words in our teaching and worship, particularly in the Protestant traditions. The "word" of God is an important and vital part of our faith. Bible passages introduce us to people and events, recount the history of God's relationship to humankind, teach us about God's ways, and guide our lives today. The words of sermons, prayers and hymns can stimulate our minds and reach into the depths of our hearts to provoke, inspire or console us. The words we use have the power to create images and define our identities and relationships. Too often, they have not sounded tidings of good news or portrayed messages of hope to people with disabilities. Indeed, too often, children and persons with learning difficulties can be excluded from full participation "because they do not understand". They, along with people who are poor, homeless, sick, in prison or struggling with addictions, are often referred to in the third person as "those" in the prayers and texts our churches frequently use. This makes it sound as if these people are not an integral part of the congregation. We need to monitor our patterns of speech that create an "us/them" relationship that casts the disabled person as the outsider, the other.

76. Metaphors can also alienate some of our brothers and sisters. Equating a lack of compassion, an unwillingness to listen, or a lack of resolve to being blind, mentally ill, deaf or paralyzed is disparaging and disempowering. By articulating our strengths or identity in terms that disparage persons who live with such physical or mental impairments, we align ourselves against them; we shut them out. Perhaps unintentionally, we project on them what is fearful or negative in ourselves and cast them as the embodiment of evil. The phrase "we are disfigured by sin" from a prayer of confession is an example of this insensitivity. It is doubtful that these words would bring solace to any person living with burn scars or facial deformity. Though we cannot change scripture passages that use such metaphors, we can find other ways to express the messages in our sermons, liturgies and hymns.

77. All these words and expressions can stimulate thinking and help clarify certain points. But to follow such discourse can be tiresome or confusing for people with little education, short attention spans, cognitive disabilities or other mental impairments. Sometimes people "hear" or comprehend God's word, and know the mystery and majesty of God's presence in their lives through a sensory experience: perception of light or colour, a picture or sculpture, a whiff of incense, silence, music, dance, a procession, a hug

or clasped hands around a circle. This sensory experience in liturgy is important to all of us, but especially to children, elderly people and persons with disabilities. It should be considered in our planning of corporate worship and its setting.

78. Many elements of worship are non-verbal, and we can be more intentional about how we incorporate them to enhance the service for everyone. There is the movement of dance, drama, hands clasped in prayer or raised in blessing, making the sign of the cross, hand-shakes and hugs, lifting the eyes, bowing the head, offering gifts, and passing the bread and cup. There are tactile elements of anointing, baptism, laying-on of hands, foot-washing, touching and vesting. We can smell the incense, wine, flowers and candles and taste the bread and wine or juice. Besides words, we hear music, clapping, bells, sighs and breathing. Centuries ago when many did not know how to read or have access to printed material, churches were filled with visual renditions of the Bible stories. There were murals, tapestries, sculpture, icons and stained glass windows. Today, some churches still have many of these visual elements and can also make use of banners, altar hangings, colourful vestments, scarves, flowers, balloons, liturgical dance and drama to portray the messages of our faith.

79. For people who do not hear well, there should be much to see; for those with very little vision, there should be much to hear. Verbal cues from the minister or liturgist are helpful to a person who is blind. Otherwise she may spend all the service trying to figure out when she should be sitting or kneeling or standing. All that needs to be said is, "You may rise" or "You may be seated". For individuals who have difficulty sitting still for very long, there should be opportunities to move. There should always be a place for some to sit even if everyone else is standing for part or all of the service. At a service where the people are seated on the floor or ground, some sort of chair or bench should be provided for people who cannot safely get down or up from such a position. Some people cannot kneel or climb steps safely, so communion needs to be brought to their level. A clear path of travel and sure footing with no stairs is necessary for those unsteady on their feet. In the arrangement of space, people who use wheelchairs need to have seating choices so that they can sit with family and friends as part of the gathered body; they should not be limited to a space way in front or far behind everyone else, or stuck out in an aisle. Several pews can be shortened to make space for wheelchairs.

80. Acoustics will be particularly important for people who are blind or hard of hearing. Individuals with limited sight rely more on their hearing, and those who are hard of hearing need good public-address systems to amplify the voice of the preacher or liturgist. Individual assistive listening devices (ALDs) that can be used with and without hearing aids may be particularly useful. Good lighting is crucial for persons with limited vision so they can make optimum use of the sight they do have. It is important for people who are deaf or hard of hearing that they can see the speaker's lips or the sign-language interpreter. A printed order of worship may be particularly helpful to people with hearing impairments. Copies can easily be produced in large print (size 18 font on a computer or enlarged on a photocopier) for people with limited vision. Large-print Bibles are available and music for a service can be enlarged on a photo-copier. Overhead projectors and computers can also be used to dis-play print material in a large format for a whole congregation. While only a small percentage of people who are blind know how to read Braille, for those who do this may be an important way to make the liturgy more accessible. Braille books, including Bibles and hymnals, take up a lot of space, so some congregations keep the pages in loose-leaf binders and remove only the ones needed for a particular service. When the service is over, the pages are put back for use another time.

81. Besides the physical accommodations such as lighting, sound systems and appropriate seating that can make a space acces-sible to everyone, we need to consider the attitudes and behaviour patterns that can create barriers for people with disabilities or cause some to feel unwelcome or left out. To feel truly welcome in the church, persons with disabilities need to see people like themselves in leadership roles. For people with disabilities to play a larger role, a faith community may need to rethink its policies about who is and who is not allowed to offer welcome, usher, or participate as ban-ner-bearer, to sing in the choir, to read the lessons and lead the prayers of the people. Is the altar area accessible to someone who uses a wheelchair or walker? Can the microphone be adjusted to different heights? Inclusion requires the conviction of the disabled person that he/she has access to leadership according to his/her abilities, attitudes and vocations, setting aside his/her complexes and frustrations.

82. Rigid codes of "acceptable" behaviour may need to be loos-ened. Just as some people cannot stand or kneel, others cannot sit still for a whole hour or more. They may need to stand or move

about because of back pain or muscle spasms or some agitation related to their disability. Some may not be able to understand the "rules" about silence and may mumble to themselves, speak out when others are quietly listening, or utter exuberant vocalizations at unexpected moments. In these situations, as with people who "make a joyful noise unto the Lord" by singing off-key, we can acquire tolerance that acknowledges such behaviour as a mild distraction rather than a great annoyance.

83. The integration of disabled people within the church gives testimony to God's love as expressed by all his sons and daughters. It can also be an example and an inspiration in those societies in which disabled people suffer from humiliating marginalization.

A church of all and for all

84. This interim statement has outlined ideals to which every society might wish to aspire. It assumes that with increasing standards of health care, people with disabilities will be so valued, accorded equality with all, cared for in the community and not in institutions or on the margins of economically competitive societies. In such regimes of provision, rehabilitation may be less important than the achievement of a certain quality of life. Such care in the community is very expensive and is, at present, beyond the means of some societies. It may even become unsustainable in political climates which espouse low-tax economies. True care in the community tends to view disabled people in a holistic way, as this statement has attempted to show, but rehabilitation often has to focus on specific problems of impairment thus reinforcing the medical model of disability. Rehabilitation may reduce care costs and offer the possibility of a livelihood and a place in society. The fight for equality and rights tends to be encouraged by those disabled people who have no need of high dependency or who have been enabled by its services to join the articulate pressure groups seeking equality and social justice.

Whether the church is involved in provision of care, rehabilitation, chaplaincy or ministry to or with disabled people, it must recognize the central assumptions of equality and dignity within the Christian message and promote it at the fore of all its work.

85. The church is by definition a place and a process of communion, open to and inviting all people without discrimination. It is a place of hospitality and a place of welcome, in the manner that Abraham and Sarah received God's messengers in the Old Testament (Gen. 18). It is an earthly reflection of a divine unity that is at

the same time worshipped as Trinity. It is a community of people with different yet complementary gifts. It is a vision of wholeness as well as of healing, of caring and of sharing at once.

Just as the body is one and has many members, so it is with Christ (1 Cor.12:12).

86. We all accept and proclaim that this is what the church is and stands for. It is the basis of our unity as Christians. Then why is it that, all too often, certain people among us and around us (usually those whom we consider as being unfamiliar or as strangers, as different or perhaps disabled) are marginalized and even excluded? Wherever this happens, even by passive omission, the church is not being what it is called to become. The church is denying its own reality. In the church, we are called to act differently. As St Paul says, the parts of the body which seem to be weaker (we should notice that he does not say "actually are weaker") are indispensable (1 Cor. 2:22).

87. When we think of people with disabilities, too often we tend to think of people who are weak and require our care. Yet, in his epistles, St Paul implies that weakness is not a characteristic of an individual or a particular group, but of the entire church. Disability does not affect only certain individuals, but involves all of us together as the people of God in a broken world. It is our world that is shattered, and each of us comprises one small, fragile and precious piece. We all hold the treasure of God's life in earthen vessels (cf. 2 Cor. 4:7). Yet we hold it; and, what is more, we hold it together. In our attitudes and actions towards one another, at all times, the guiding principle must be the conviction that we are incomplete, we are less than whole, without the gifts and talents of all people. We are not a full community without one another. Responding to and fully including people with disabilities is not an option for the churches of Christ. It is the church's defining characteristic.

88. Interdependence is the key here. Even though the secular world stresses independence, we are called to live as a community dependent on God and on one another. No one of us should be considered a burden for the rest; and no one of us is simply a burden-bearer. "We all bear one another's burdens in order to fulfil the law of Christ" (Gal. 6:2).

89. Perhaps it is the starting point in our attitude and in our response that requires redirection at this point. Perhaps we should consider not simply the particular needs, but also the unique gifts of all people in the community. In another passage on the church as

the body of Christ, St Paul writes, "For as in one body we have many members, and not all members have the same function, so we, though we are many, are one body in Christ, and individually we are members one of another..." (Rom. 12:4-5).

Every child and every adult, those with disabilities and those without disabilities alike, will bring specific and special gifts and talents to the church. This is the challenge addressed to us all. Thus we can truly be "A Church of All and for All" – a church which reflects God's intention for humankind.

May we who are made in your image, O God, mirror your compassion, creativity and imagination as we work to reshape our society, our buildings, our programmes, and our worship so that all may participate. In you we are no longer alone, but united in one body. Trusting in your wisdom and grace, we pray gratefully in Jesus' name.

The Risk Book Series from WCC Publications deals with issues of crucial importance to Christians around the world today. Each volume contains well-informed and provocative perspectives on current concerns in the ecumenical movement, written in an easy-to-read style for a general church audience.

Although any Risk book may be ordered separately, those who subscribe to the series are assured of receiving all four volumes published during the year by airmail immediately upon publication – at a substantial savings on the price for individual copies.

If you wish to subscribe to the Risk series, please send your name and address to WCC Publications, P.O.Box 2100, 1211 Geneva 2, Switzerland, publications@wcc-coe.org, fax +41.22.798.13.46. Subscription prices for 2004 are: Sw.Fr.58.00, US$35.00, £24.50, €38.00. Some of the titles published recently in the series are:

Hans-Ruedi Weber
Walking on the Way
Biblical Signposts

In this refreshing reflection on key biblical texts, the author employs literary and historical analysis in discussing the great festivals of the ecclesiastical year and the important periods in between. Additionally, he draws on the work of artists, especially painters and weavers, interpreting images and symbols they use.

Hans-Ruedi Weber was formerly director for biblical studies at the WCC and professor at the Graduate School of Ecumenical Studies at Bossey, near Geneva.
110pp., CHF17.00, €11.00, £6.95, US$9.95

Simon Oxley
Creative Ecumenical Education
Learning from One Another

This book maintains that everyday encounters and planned interactions can become the foundation for ecumenical learning and offer a powerful alternative to formal and book-based education. It explores ways in which to encourage this creative, informal approach alongside and within formal education.

Simon Oxley, formerly general secretary of the National Christian Education Council in the UK, is currently team coordinator of the WCC's Educational and Ecumenical Formation team.
156pp., CHF17.00, €11.00, £6.95, US$9.95

Ian M. Fraser
Many Cells – One Body
Stories from Small Christian Communities

In these extended families of fellowship and service, the author discerns the work of one Spirit in a multiplicity of circumstances. He argues that this movement's departure from convention should be regarded not as a threat to traditional leadership but as a gift to the whole people of God.

Ian Fraser, who has been in contact with SCCs for over fifty years, has served on the staff of the Church of Scotland and the WCC.

118pp., CHF16.00, €9.95, £6.95, US$9.95

Samuel Kobia
The Courage to Hope
The Roots for a New Vision and the Calling of the Church in Africa
The author examines the reality and potential of contemporary Africa, and affirms that the African sense of identity growing from ancient traditions provides a rich spiritual resource for shaping a new Africa. He advocates for a transformation of consciousness based in the reaffirmation of human dignity.

Samuel Kobia is the sixth general secretary of the WCC.

230pp., CHF24.00, €14.50, £10.95, US$16.95

Jill Tabart
Coming to Consensus
A Case Study for the Churches
From the Uniting Church in Australia, to Methodist bishops' conferences in North America, to the governing committees of the WCC, Christian deliberative bodies are exploring new methods of making decisions. A case study of one church's development of a non-confrontational governing process, *Coming to Consensus* is a resource for church councils at every level as they seek an authentically Christian method for discussing contested issues and discerning ways to move forward together.

Jill Tabart served as president of the national assembly of the Uniting Church in Australia at the time consensus procedures were introduced.

90pp., CHF14.00, €8.95, £5.95, US$10.95

Edward Dommen
How Just Is the Market Economy?
This theologically informed study in economic ethics focuses on the "world market" as an ideology, a formal theory and a practical device. It analyzes the tendency of economists to elaborate and impose market theory as dogma. Such approaches are contrasted with principles of justice found in the Bible. The author concludes that market mechanisms must be supplemented by additional tools to ensure that world needs may be fairly and correctly met.

Edward Dommen is an economist, retired following two decades of service to the United Nations Conference on Trade and Development (UNCTAD).

116pp., CHF18.00. €11.50, £7.95, US$13.95